Footsteps 2
The Cream of Walks in North-East Wiltshire

Chris Cole

First published in the United Kingdom in 2008 by
The Hobnob Press, PO Box 1838, East Knoyle, Salisbury SP3 6FA

British Library Cataloguing in Publication Data
A catalogue record for this book is available from the British Library.

ISBN 978-0-946418-80-0

Typeset in 10/12 pt ITC Officina Serif and Futura
Typesetting and origination by John Chandler
Printed in Great Britain by Salisbury Printing Company Ltd, Salisbury

*The cover design is based on artwork by David Cousins and a
photograph by Chris Cole*

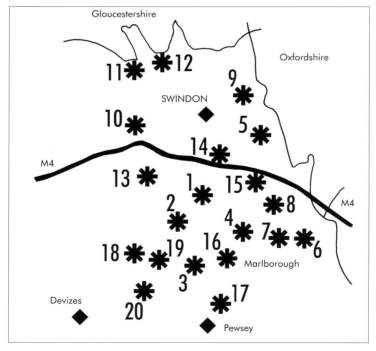

Approximate locations of the walks in relation to local towns

Contents

About the Author

Chris Cole was born in 1948 in the Cambridgeshire Fens. He became interested in walking and photography at an early age, and during a 31-year career in the banking industry, managed to find some spare time to write for magazines. After taking early retirement, he became a full-time freelance writer, and has since supplied features and pictures to a number of different publications. In 2000 he began writing monthly walking articles for *Wiltshire Life* magazine, and excerpts from some of those walks appear in this book. Others are new or variations. He also contributed to the first volume of *Footsteps* which covered South Wiltshire.

Together with his wife, Ann, who was born in Marlborough, he walks extensively around the county on a regular basis. Apart from Wiltshire, his favourite walking areas are the North of England and the coast of Cornwall.

Introduction

Rolling chalk downland, tranquil river valleys, ancient woodlands, and unusual geological formations; the landscape of North-East Wiltshire has all of these, and more. Add a rich variety of prehistoric monuments and architectural styles, plus wildlife, wildflowers and local history, and you have a wealth of interest to accompany any walk in this part of the county. This book brings together these various components in a series of local walks that should appeal to a wide cross-section of readers, with varying degrees of experience.

As well as the obvious health benefits, walking is an ideal way of exploring new areas and enjoying some delightful countryside. In this respect Wiltshire has much to offer, yet is frequently overlooked. Consequently, you will not be competing for space on a crowded footpath; indeed you may go for miles without seeing another soul – peace and tranquillity are not hard to find.

In preparing the descriptions of the routes, I have tried to strike a balance that will suit everyone. Instructions are printed in bold type within numbered paragraphs that correspond to the accompanying sketch maps. These maps are intended only as a general guide, and should not be regarded as a substitute for the Ordnance Survey Explorer maps that are an essential accessory for anyone walking in unfamiliar territory. For identification purposes, grid references are provided at key locations.

No specialist equipment is required, but a decent pair of walking boots is recommended, as well as a waterproof, and additional layers on colder days. It should be remembered that Wiltshire hilltops are exposed locations, with little shelter from inclement weather. A few of the walks include steep gradients or main road crossings, while others may be prone to flooding after heavy rain. Wherever possible, known trouble spots are highlighted.

While all the routes have been checked for accuracy, local conditions can change over time, and occasionally rights of way may be amended. No responsibility can be accepted for any errors or ambiguities; anyone undertaking these walks does so at their own risk. Walking should be an enjoyable experience, and I hope this book will help readers to discover new territories, or renew some old acquaintances. In doing so, please remember to observe the country code by shutting gates, keeping to permitted paths, and respecting the environment for the benefit of wildlife and others.

My grateful thanks go to John Chandler for encouraging me to write this book, and to Ann, my wife, who accompanied me on each of these walks.

Chris Cole

Further reading – general

In addition to the publications listed at the end of individual chapters, the following books are recommended for readers who want to learn more about this area of Wiltshire:

Bailey, Justin, 2006, *Lost Railways of Wiltshire*. (Countryside Books)

Chandler, John, 2001, *Marlborough and Eastern Wiltshire*. (Hobnob Press)

Maggs, Colin G, 1967, *The Midland & South Western Junction Railway*. (David & Charles)

Marshman, Michael, 1987, *The Wiltshire Village Book*. (Countryside Books)

Watts, Ken, 2001, *Exploring Historic Wiltshire: Volume 1: North*. (Ex Libris Press)

Watts, Ken, 2002, *Figures in a Wiltshire Scene*. (Hobnob Press)

Watts, Ken, 2003, *The Marlborough Downs*. (Ex Libris Press)

WILTSHIRE LIFE. Some of the walks featured in this book, or variations of them, have previously appeared in past issues of Wiltshire Life, the monthly county magazine refounded by Mark Allen in 1995. Published by A&D Media Ltd at Dinton, near Salisbury, the magazine is available from various outlets around the county.

For details of subscription rates contact the publisher on Freephone 0800 137201, or visit their website www.wiltshirelife.co.uk.

1 **Where it all Began**

Barbury Castle

(8 miles/12.8 km) or (5 miles/8 km)

(OS Explorer 157)

Many years ago, Barbury Castle was the first Wiltshire hilltop I visited after moving to this part of the country, so it is more than appropriate that it should appear at the beginning of this book. Since that first visit I have returned many times, and in all weathers, from hot blazing sunshine to torrential rain. The most memorable, however, has to be a day in January 2005, when overnight snow had left a white blanket over the high ground. Lower down, thick sheets of ice covered the access road, making it impossible to drive up the final gradient until a thaw set in later in the day. Early that morning I had to be content with parking elsewhere, and walking the extra distance. In such pristine conditions, beneath a clear blue sky, that was no hardship.

Whatever the weather, you will enjoy this special place. Ice permitting, access to the country park is easy, by following the no through road from the B4005 near Wroughton. Look out for the brown signs at nearby road junctions. At the top a large car park looks out across Swindon; parking is free, but the gate is locked overnight. At peak times a café is open for refreshments.

A visit to the nearby hillfort is optional, but our walk sets off in the opposite direction, and is mainly on byways and bridleways, some of which are deeply rutted. Throughout the route the height varies from around 140 to 260 metres above sea level, so gradients are inevitable, although no severe climbing is involved.

1 From the entrance to the car park (SU 157761), walk back down the road until you reach a gate and stile on the right-hand side. Here you will find an open access roundel and a waymarker for the Millennium Trail. A short distance beyond the gate is an upright sarsen stone commemorating two local authors.

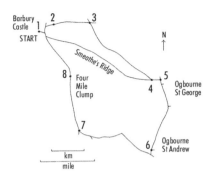

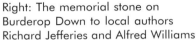

Right: The memorial stone on Burderop Down to local authors Richard Jefferies and Alfred Williams

We shall be learning about Richard Jefferies and Alfred Williams in later chapters. Both were born on the outskirts of Swindon, and spent many hours walking around these hills, about which they enthused passionately in their writings. The inscription to Richard Jefferies is an excerpt from his book *The Story of my Heart*, while the dedication to Alfred Williams was taken from his *Songs in Wiltshire*.

2 Continue past the memorial stone to follow the multi-rutted track along the fence line. Cross two stiles and fork right where a bridleway joins from the left. Where the track bends around, look for a gate on your right-hand side, bearing a blue arrow (SU 171764).

3 Go through the gate and follow the edge of the large field, alongside a line of fir trees. On reaching a farm track by a large group of trees, continue along it briefly, then fork right at the bridleway sign to climb onto another rutted field edge. After a while the track narrows between hedgerows, then widens as it approaches a junction beside a gate (SU 189747).

We have now reached the Ridgeway National Trail, which is clearly waymarked by the acorn symbol. Also on the gate here is a sign forbidding entry to all motor vehicles, a recent introduction to control the damage previously caused to the Ridgeway. At this point the national trail does not follow the original or ancient Ridgeway, which takes a more direct course from Barbury Castle to cross the A346 just south of Chiseldon. We shall be discussing the Ridgeway more fully in the next chapter.

4 To return to Barbury Castle by the 5-mile route over Smeathe's Ridge, turn right through this gate and follow the rutted hillside track. The route is clearly waymarked as it gradually climbs up to, and along the full length of the wide grass escarpment, with extensive views. Follow it for 2 miles (3.2 km), then at the top go through the gate and turn right to return to the car park.

5 Otherwise, bear left along the Ridgeway towards Ogbourne St George. At the road turn right along it for 100m to the first bend, where a wide dirt track continues straight on, signposted Liddington Castle 6.1 miles, (even though Liddington Castle is actually behind us at this point!) Follow the Ridgeway for 800m to a byway junction, where it turns left (SU 194737). We continue straight ahead on a chalk track that may be slippery when wet.

6 Entering Ogbourne St Andrew, bear right along the road, then right again at the junction to pass the church. This is a no through road that ends at a large barn (SU 180730). Turn left in front of it onto a wide track that climbs up to a second barn on the exposed hilltop.

7 Go to the right of the barn and turn right beside the gallops fencing. After 400m we arrive at a multi-track junction beside a signpost (SU 168731). Bear right to continue on a wide rutted track, heading directly to a group of trees on the horizon.

Bridleway above Ogbourne St Andrew

Ahead of us is Four Mile Clump, an isolated group of trees that is clearly visible for some distance in all directions. It takes its name from the old milestone beside the track, situated exactly 4 miles (6.4 km) from Marlborough. The track we are following is the original Swindon–Marlborough coach road. Its uneven surface gives us a clue to the terrible discomfort endured by the coach passengers. Add to that the isolated downland setting, with its exposure to the weather, and we have some idea what travel was like in past times. Cattle drovers who also passed this way would not have been at all concerned by the state of the road, but they were certainly not pleased about the toll charges that were introduced after it was turnpiked in 1762.

A century later the road was regularly used by a younger generation. The railways were late in reaching Marlborough, and for the first 20 or 30 years after Marlborough College was established in 1843, Swindon was the nearest convenient station. Consequently at the start and finish of each school term the boys had to travel back and forth to Swindon by horse-drawn bus. Several years later, one Marlborough schoolboy was still using the old road on a regular basis. Both Barbury Castle and Four Mile Clump were favourite haunts of Charles Sorley, who gained immense pleasure and inspiration for his poetry, by walking and running across the Marlborough Downs. Frequently his verses mention locations we can easily recognize today.

> Away to rightward I descry
> My Barbury ensconced in sky
> For underneath the Ogbourne twins,
> And at my feet the thyme and whins,
> The grasses with their little crowns
> Of gold, the lovely Aldbourne downs . . .

We shall be visiting the Aldbourne downs in later chapters, and walking in more of Sorley's footsteps. In the meantime our walk from Barbury Castle is almost finished, but if time permits a visit to the hillfort will be rewarded with more extensive views, including along the Ridgeway towards Hackpen hill, the location for our next walk.

8 From Four Mile Clump continue along the track for another mile (1.6 km) to return to the car park at Barbury Castle.

The ramparts on Barbury Castle hillfort

IRON AGE HILLFORTS (800 BC – 43 AD). Barbury Castle is one of around 3,000 hillforts built across Britain during the period immediately before the Roman occupation (43 AD – 410 AD). As their name suggests, most were created for defensive purposes, although some were used solely for settlement and stock-holding. Their sizes range from just half an acre to over 700 acres. Built around 500 BC, the hillfort at Barbury Castle covers an area of 11 acres, and falls into the category known as Bivallate, meaning that it was enclosed by a double bank and ditch. Facing it on the opposite side of the Og valley, the hillfort on Liddington Hill has a single bank, or Univallate. Between them they guarded the head of the valley, a key route into Wessex from the Thames Valley. Consequently, they remained occupied during the post-Roman period, when Saxon invaders were advancing across southern England. Numerous battles took place during the 5th and 6th centuries. In 556 AD one of them was fought on the lower slopes of Barbury Castle, which was subsequently named by the Saxons as *Beranburgh* (or Bera's Hill). Precise details of the battle are sketchy, but in his *Villages of the White Horse,* Alfred Williams provides us with an interesting account: 'Here the Britons, burning to avenge their defeat of a few years earlier, assembled a mighty host of their bravest warriors to oppose the Saxons. But neither choice of ground, nor the tradition of Roman tactics, nor heroic Celtic valour, could withstand the terrible impetuosity of the West Saxon foot, and when the sun set, after a stout hand-to-hand fight that had lasted all day, Ceawlin was victor; the kingdom of Wessex was firmly established.'

By their very nature, hillforts occupied elevated positions that gave early warning of an approaching enemy. Today they provide us with extensive views across the surrounding landscape, and this is certainly true at Barbury Castle.

Further reading:

Hogg, A H A, 1975, *Hill-forts in Britain*. (Hart-Davis, MacGibbon)

Forde-Johnston, James, 1976, *Hillforts of the Iron Age in England and Wales*. (Liverpool University Press)

Williams, Geoffrey, 1993, *The Iron Age Hillforts of England: a visitors guide*. (Images)

OPEN ACCESS LAND. Authorised by the Countryside & Rights of Way Act, open access land is for walking only. Other outdoor activities are prohibited, including cycling, horse-riding, camping, and driving any form of vehicle. However, existing public rights of way are not affected. If in doubt, keep to designated footpaths, bridleways and byways. Dogs must be kept on a short lead between 1st March and 31st July, and at all times near livestock. Some open access land contains prohibited areas, most of which are obvious, for example, railways and airfields. In Wiltshire the most common exception likely to be encountered is cultivated fields, and land within 20 metres of a house or farm building. For full details of the regulations visit www.countryside.gov.uk.

2 Land of Sheep and Sarsens

Hackpen Hill and Fyfield Down

(6.75 miles/10.8 km) or (9.25miles/14.8 km)

(OS Explorer 157)

A choice of routes across exposed downland ridges allows for a last minute change of plan if the weather turns nasty. There is no shelter in this high terrain, but a fine day will offer ample reward, with extensive views and an opportunity to explore some unusual landscapes that many have likened to the surface of the Moon. You will be intrigued by the sarsen stones lying scattered all over Fyfield Down, their curious shapes said to resemble sheep, hence their nickname of grey wethers. This is not the only strange name you will encounter, for this is a land of mystery. Starting with an easy but lengthy stroll along the Ridgeway, we then follow various tracks, bridleways and byways across typical Wiltshire downland. One of them is an old coach road used by well known personalities of the day. Here too you may have encounters with wildlife, or see snowdrops and bluebells in bloom.

1 Begin the walk from the car park on Hackpen Hill where the Ridgeway crosses the Broad Hinton to Marlborough road (SU 129747). Follow the signpost towards Overton Hill.

At 272m above sea level, Hackpen features in the top ten of Wiltshire's highest hills. Consequently the views are extensive, and its western slope provides an ideal location for a chalk carving. Best seen as you approach along the road from Broad Hinton, Hackpen white horse was cut in 1838 to celebrate the Coronation of Queen Victoria. At about the same time, another

white horse was cut on Rockley
Down, barely two miles (3.2 km)
away along the Marlborough road.
Unlike its stable mate on Hackpen,
this horse faced north, and would
have been visible to travellers on
the old Swindon to Marlborough
coach road, near Four Mile Clump.
Little is known about its origins,
and it seems to have quickly
vanished, before suddenly re-
appearing in 1948, when it was
exposed by ploughing. For a few
days it became a celebrity,

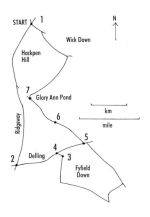

attracting media interest from around the world. Aerial
photographs were hastily taken, fearing that it would soon
disappear again. It did, and has not been seen since.

2 Follow the Ridgeway south for 2.5 miles (4 km) to its
junction with the Wessex Ridgeway on Overton Down (SU
125708). A notice board here welcomes you to Fyfield Down
nature reserve. Turn left through the gate and follow the
wide grass path across the open down. Go through more
gates to cross the gallops, then downhill on a gravel track.
At the bottom follow the track around left, and climb up to
the sheep pens near a derelict house at Delling (SU
136711).

This ancient highway is often shown on maps as Green Street,
the name displayed on the road sign where it enters Avebury.
Its origins are uncertain, but at some point it was taken over
by coach travellers as an early route of the London–Bath Road,
known locally as the Old London Way. Beside Delling Copse deep
ruts can still be seen alongside the main track, where coach
wheels dug into the surface as they fought for grip on the
hillside. This was a remote, bleak and desolate place in those
days, where travellers were at the mercy of the weather and
highwaymen. Nevertheless the dangers failed to deter royalty
and other important people from travelling this way to visit
the spa waters at Bath.

Today it is still an isolated place, with no shelter from wind
or rain. But this isolation attracts all sorts of wildlife, and on a
fine, calm day you may well hear a skylark singing to its mate,
or see crows, kestrels and buzzards in the air. In places, the
down almost resembles a green lunar landscape, littered with
sarsen stones of all shapes and sizes, many half buried like

Multi-shaped Sarsen boulders on Clatford Down

prehistoric tombstones. Here too you will find a large display of gorse, a bush that tolerates any type of soil, and therefore can be found almost anywhere in the country. Although at its best in spring, yellow gorse can flower at any time of year, climate change notwithstanding. For centuries it was used as fuel, for it produces intense heat with minimal ash residue. In Ireland it was once considered so important to the rural economy that tithes were levied on its various uses, which included adding flavour to whiskey, and even curing snake bite.

SARSENS ON FYFIELD DOWN. Dating from the Tertiary period of around 50 million years ago, sarsen stones were created by the fusing together of sand and silica. Sometime later they were transported to Fyfield Down by glacial action, and came to the surface when the softer chalk above them was washed away. The result is a very hard, dense rock that our ancestors used to create the great monuments at Stonehenge and Avebury. It occurs in various places across southern England, and sarsens from Buckinghamshire were used to build much of Windsor Castle. The main deposits are now in Wiltshire, largely across the Marlborough Downs, where they can be found either on, or just below the surface. When Samuel Pepys travelled from Avebury to Marlborough in 1668 he wrote in his diary, '. . . it was prodigious to see how full the Downes are of great stones; and all along the valleys, stones of considerable bigness, most of them growing certainly out of the ground so thick as to cover the ground...' Then in 1936 H J Massingham referred to

Fyfield Down as '. . . the Valley of the Desolation of the Rocks, for it is strewn with a multitude of sarsen stones, great and small and half embedded in the sweet turf.' During the intervening years much had changed here. For centuries sarsen had been a building material for houses, churches, walls and paving, with many examples in the surrounding villages. Its dense structure made it difficult to cut, but stonemasons in Buckinghamshire had devised ways of doing so. In 1840 they discovered the freely available source of raw material scattered all over the downs, and promptly moved their business to Wiltshire. Then during the early part of the 20th century concern began to grow about the rapid disappearance of the sarsens. As a result, in 1907 two areas of land were purchased by the National Trust at Lockeridge and Piggledene. The stones' greatest saviour, however, was the development of the concrete industry, which effectively made sarsen obsolete as a building material. The stonemasons ceased trading around 1939, when some of the last sarsens taken from Fyfield Down were delivered to Windsor Castle for repairs.

Theories about the origins of the name include a link with the Saracens, meaning foreigners or strangers, although it is not clear who these foreigners might be. Some suggest it is the alien sandstone rocks themselves, found in a predominantly limestone terrain; others attribute it to the stonemasons who came from outside the area. A more plausible explanation comes from the Saxon words 'sar', meaning troublesome, and 'stan', meaning stone. The confusion does not end there. For years the sarsen stones on the downs have been referred to as 'grey wethers', amid claims that they are easily mistaken for sheep lying on the ground. There may be an element of truth in this comparison, at least at a distance, although close inspection reveals that most of the stones are now covered by mosses and rare lichens, one of which occurs only on sarsen. Whilst mainly grey, sarsens can vary in colour and some have been stained by iron oxide that turns them reddish-brown. It certainly confused John Aubrey when he saw them in the 17th century. In his *Natural History of Wiltshire* he wrote '. . . some are a kind of dirty red, towards porphyry; some perfect white; some dusky white; some blew, like deep blew marle; some of a kind of olive greenish colour; but generally they are whitish.' Today Fyfield Down national nature reserve contains the UK's largest collection of sarsen stones — some 25,000 of them.

3 To inspect more of the sarsen stone landscape of Fyfield Down, and extend the walk by 2.5 miles (4 km), go through the gate by the sheep pens at Delling, then almost immediately leave the main track by bearing right on a grass path beside a fence. At the trees, go through the gate on your right, and follow the fence as it goes around the perimeter of the open access land. After 500m a track forks left along the valley bottom, while the fence climbs up to the field boundary (SU 136703), then turns left to run parallel at a higher level. Choose either route, for after 800m they merge and bear right along the valley floor to pass an English Nature information board. Continue to a gate at the far end (SU 150698), but do not go through it. Instead, turn left uphill beside the fence. At the top turn right with the fence, and follow it to another gate. Bear left to a second gate, then left again along a wide track signed as cycle routes 4 & 45. Follow this track for 1500m to a T-junction by a covered reservoir. Turn left for 100m to a signpost towards Hackpen (SU 143714). Rejoin the main route and continue from point 5.

4 To bypass the extended route over Fyfield Down, go through the gate by the sheep pens and continue along the main track for 700m. Then after leaving the nature reserve by another gate and notice, proceed to the signpost on the left pointing towards Hackpen (SU 143714). Rejoin the extended route.

Hackpen white horse

5 Turn here towards Hackpen, and cross the open down to a gate at the entrance to Totterdown Wood (SU 139718). Go through the gate and follow the track as it meanders through the trees.

Expect the narrow path to be muddy, even in relatively dry conditions, for this is a damp place. Consequently, moss grows everywhere, including on the sarsen stones that litter the woodland floor. Look out too for fine displays of snowdrops and bluebells. Bricks were once made here, and the derelict stone building was probably part of that industry.

6 Emerging from the other side of the wood, continue straight ahead on a rutted track, then over a crossroads and fork slightly right along the edge of the next field. Within a few minutes we arrive at another junction where two ponds are hidden in the trees (SU 128726).

This is Glory Ann pond, or to be more correct, ponds, created when clay was extracted to make the bricks in Totterdown Wood. A nearby pile of rubble indicates the spot where a barn once stood, and until the 19th century two cottages were also occupied, at a time when drovers stopped here to water their cattle. Despite much speculation and research, the origin of the unusual name of this place still remains a mystery, with some theories linking it to the Orient.

7 The Ridgeway is just 400m ahead, if you wish to return to Hackpen by a direct route. If so, take the left-hand track. Otherwise, turn right between two fence posts as indicated by the blue arrow. Then fork left onto a wide rutted track. Follow the fence around to the right, then after 100m fork left at the intersection, waymarked by a yellow arrow on the post. Go past some bushes and stay beside the fence all the way to Wick Down Farm. Beyond the gate, continue through the farmyard and exit on the road that bears around to the right. Older maps show a different route here, which should be ignored. Instead, follow the main farm road for a further 300m to a junction just before a bend (SU 139738). Turn left on a wide track, signed to the Ridgeway. After passing Fortnight bungalow, the gravel track climbs steeply for a while, finally emerging on the road just 400m from the car park on Hackpen Hill. Turn left along the grass verge.

THE RIDGEWAY. It is important to make a clear distinction between the Ancient Ridgeway and the present day Ridgeway National Trail, which officially opened in 1973. Always regarded as our oldest road, the Ancient Ridgeway probably dates back 5,000 years. It developed as a means of communication and trade between the many hilltop communities of southern England. At the time few people lived in the valleys, which were still largely forested and undrained. A significant proportion of the population occupied the elevated plateau of Salisbury Plain, and the Ridgeway provided a high level link to other parts of the country, maybe as far as the Dorset coast in one direction, and to North Norfolk in the other. Over the centuries much of the route has been lost, but the section from the Chilterns to the Wiltshire Downs remains largely intact. Consequently in recent years a good part of it has been adopted as a National Trail that starts at Ivinghoe Beacon in Buckinghamshire, and ends beside the A4 on Overton Hill – a distance of 87 miles (139 km). Primarily the route follows the top of the chalk downland ridge, although in a few locations it has to make minor diversions. Most sections now prohibit motor vehicles in order to prevent surface damage. As we shall see in chapter 5, the Ridgeway National Trail is just one of four long distance footpaths that now make up the original route of the Ancient, or Greater Ridgeway.

Further reading:

Quinlan, Ray, 2003, *The Greater Ridgeway*. (Cicerone)
Andrew, Martin, 2001, *Chilterns & Ridgeway*. (Harper Collins)
Bergamar, Kate, 1997, *Discovering hill figures*. (Shire)
Marples, Morris, 1991, *White Horses and other hill figures*. (Alan Sutton)

3 The Nation's Favourite

West Woods and Lockeridge

(5.5 miles/8.8 km)

(OS Explorer 157)

Or littering for the fields of May
Lady-smocks a-bleaching lay,
And like a skylit water stood
The bluebells in the azured wood.

(A E Housman)

Voted by the public as our favourite wildflower, the humble bluebell produces a display that is unique to this country. Shaded  *by the canopy of countless trees, woodland floors turn blue each spring as nature unveils one of her glorious spectacles. And one of the best places to see it is in West Woods, an offshoot of Savernake Forest.*
During the first few weeks of the year, snowdrops, wood anemones, and primroses add occasional splashes of colour amongst the fallen leaves and broken branches. All around green shoots start to penetrate the surface, and by early April a faint blue haze appears as vast numbers of bluebells slowly reveal their fragrant bell-shaped blooms. As the month progresses the colour intensifies, usually reaching a peak at the beginning of May. In future years, however, this timescale may become less predictable as global warming continues to upset the life-cycle of many of our flowering plants.

1 Start from the car park in West Woods (SU 162666), which is accessed from the minor road that runs through Clatford Bottom. Walk back along the entrance road for about 100m to a signpost where a bridleway joins from the left, and a footpath goes right. Turn right on the uphill woodland path, then merge with a wider track for a short distance until it bends around to the right. At this point we join the **White Horse Trail**, and follow its distinctive waymarkers for a while. As indicated, turn left beside a line of fir trees, then fork right at another waymarker post. In the trees, go past a post with a yellow top, and exit onto the road near a farm. Cross over onto a permissive path, at first beside a broken fence, then along a ditch and bank, just inside the perimeter of the forest.

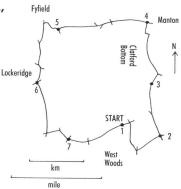

Along here vast swathes of bluebells grow all over the woodland floor, as well as on the bank and across the path, where it is sometimes difficult to avoid treading on them. A few weeks earlier clusters of snowdrops provide winter colour, and occasionally a rogue white bluebell can be seen flowering at the same time.

The bank and ditch are part of the Wansdyke, a gigantic linear earthwork built during the Dark Ages to repel hostile invaders. At this point it is much diminished, although its passage through the woods can easily be followed. Between here and the main expanse of Savernake Forest, short sections of it still exist, but are not generally accessible. Its most impressive remains are elsewhere, and we shall be visiting them in a later chapter.

2 At the end of the wood (SU 169664) an isolated stile stands at a footpath crossing, where there are several yellow arrows. Turn left, still following the edge of the wood, until you reach a gate on your left, to emerge on an open hillside, overlooking the entrance to the car park. Turn right along the top of the hillside, keeping close to the fence/hedgerow. Do not descend. Cross a stile, and continue ahead as far as a short line of trees coming up the hillside. Look in the bushes to locate a stile in the fence. Climb the low bank, and fork left to cross an open field diagonally on a faint path. Aim for the left-hand end of the line of trees, where a signpost stands at a path junction (SU 168675).

3 Bear left along a wide rutted track between two large fields. Reaching more trees, where the track turns left, continue straight on, briefly alongside the field, then through the wood. More bluebells grow here. Emerging into the open, go around the bushes in front of you to locate a stile, where an arrow points left. Continue along the edge of the field, with a hedgerow on your left. At the end, go over two stiles near a house, and immediately turn left around the perimeter of the field, beside a hedge/fence. At the bottom of the field go over the stile to emerge on Manton Road (SU 166685).

4 Turn left along the narrow road to Clatford crossroads, then proceed for another 100m until the road bends left towards Lockeridge. Here a bridleway sign points straight ahead along a rough track. Go past the first two houses, then straight on towards another where the main track goes right. Before reaching the third house, go through the gate on your right to enter the field, as directed. Follow the fence to exit the field by a second gate, and proceed along a wide enclosed path. Ignore other track turnings. At a junction beside three gates, continue straight on to follow the edge of the field to a thatched cottage. Go through the gate, and along the gravel drive in front of the cottage, to exit onto the narrow lane. Turn right over the river bridge (SU 151684).

5 Follow the road to a double bend beside the old dairy, where it enters Fyfield. As the road turns right around a thatched cottage, look left for a footpath sign. Go through the opening to follow a fence-lined path to a kissing gate. Proceed along the edge of two fields, and exit onto a tarmac drive beside a white thatched cottage and stables. Continue to the road, and turn left along the pavement until it ends beside Lockeridge school. Then carry on beside the road to the village green (SU 147675).

Some might claim that Lockeridge does not qualify to be called a village because it has no church, whereas nearby Fyfield does. On the other hand, Lockeridge does have a school and pub, the latter proudly displaying its unusual, but not entirely unique, name 'Who'd a thought it?' Explanations vary, one theory linking it to past rivalry between the landlord and the baker, with the baker subsequently taking over the pub. An alternative story is that the publican was so surprised to be granted a licence, as the local magistrates had a reputation for being hard hearted. Further on, a distinctive line of pollarded lime trees stand beside the road like sentries, then around the next corner is the village green. Directly opposite is Lockeridge Dene, a site purchased by the National Trust in 1907 to help preserve local deposits of sarsen stones.

6 **After making a slight detour to visit the National Trust site, return to the road junction, and turn left at the Huish bridleway sign. An enclosed path climbs steadily to a gate beside gallops. Continue straight on beside the fence, still climbing to the top of the field. Enter the wood through another gate, and proceed on a wide track until you reach a junction where there are several waymarkers on a post (SU 149665). Take the first turning on your left, to another bridleway signpost in front of the lodge. Turn right between the bushes onto a stony downhill track. At the bottom is another bridleway crossing and signpost (SU 152664).**

In 1920 a stone crushing plant was established in the woods here, to provide ballast material for road surfacing. Much of it was used on the nearby Bath Road (A4), which was undergoing a programme of improvements at the time. However, sarsen chippings proved to be unsuitable for the purpose, and the operators quickly went out of business.

Sarsen stones at Lockeridge Dene

7 Cross over the junction, and bear left steeply uphill on another stony track. At the top is another bridleway junction with several waymarkers. Continue straight on along a wider track. Bear left at the next intersection, still on the main track, and follow it all the way back to the car park.

BLUEBELLS (*Hyacinthoides non-scripta*). Although bluebells can be found in other parts of northern Europe, almost half the world's population grows in the British Isles, mostly in the semi-shade of deciduous woodland. Confusingly, in Scotland the name bluebell is used to describe the harebell, while the bluebell is known as wild hyacinth. Bluebell woods have been around since at least the 16th century, and take many years to fully develop into the extensive carpets such as those in West Woods. The plants complete their flowering cycle before the trees come into full leaf – thus making maximum use of available light. Then as the tree canopy closes, and the bluebell leaves smother the woodland floor, other competing plants are unable to become established, thus allowing the bluebells to thrive. Careful forestry management also contributes to the bluebells' expansion. Precisely what effect climate change may have on this finely-tuned balance remains to be seen, but already our native bluebell is having to compete with the Spanish bluebell that was introduced as a garden plant in 1680. Over the past century these more robust varieties have escaped into the wild, and many can be seen growing alongside the native species in West Woods. Perhaps more than any other flower, the bluebell is a clear sign that spring has arrived, even if the weather often suggests otherwise.

Further reading:

Gillam, Beatrice, 1993, *The Wiltshire Flora*. (Pisces).
Tanner, Heather & Robin, 1981, *Woodland Plants*. (Robin Garton).

4 The Sign of a Great Poet

Poulton Downs and the Ogbournes

(7 miles/11.2 km)   or   (8.25 miles/13.2 km)

(OS Explorer 157)

On the Poulton Downs, a couple of miles north-east of Marlborough, stands a wooden signpost. At its base is a sarsen stone, engraved with the letters CHS, the initials of one of our greatest war poets, who during his time at Marlborough College, spent many hours wandering these lonely hills. This walk explores some of the area mentioned in his poetry, a landscape that is predominantly farmland, with extensive views and opportunities to see wildlife. Much of the route is on byways, with some early climbing, as well as a level section along the trackbed of an old railway line. An option to extend the distance is available, without missing any of the main highlights. There are no refreshment facilities en route, but a short detour can be made to pubs in Ogbourne St George and Ogbourne St Andrew.

1 Start at the layby beside the A346 at Bay Bridge, one mile (1.6 km) north of Marlborough (SU 187709). Near the entrance is a stile between a gate and the edge of the adjacent golf course. Turn right to follow the hedgerow behind the layby, then fork left across the corner of the field to locate a gap in the trees. A plank bridge crosses the stream. Continue over the next field, through another hedgerow, then along the fence line to exit onto a driveway just before the buildings. Go past the stables and exit between gates to continue along the village road to the A346. Carefully cross over onto the byway directly opposite. The uphill track goes around to the right and over the old railway path at cross-tracks on a raised bank (previously a bridge here). Remember this location as we shall return to it later (SU 189716).

2 The chalk track now climbs gradually, but not too steeply, for 700m. At the top there are views across the Ogbourne villages and beyond to Wroughton airfield and the Foxhill transmitter. Passing a belt of trees, the track levels out, and we continue in the same direction until we reach a junction with a narrow road at a farm (SU 209717).

On the verge here is the traditional wooden signpost that Charles Sorley passed many times, and included in his poems:

> I may not think on those dear lands
> (O far away and long ago!)
> Where the old battered sign-post stands,
> And silently the four roads go.

The Sorley signpost

In the recent past the signpost met with an accident, and on various visits I have seen it either lying on the ground or propped up against the tree. Fortunately it has since been repaired, so unless it meets with further misfortunes, you should be able to rely upon it for directions. At this point we have to choose which route to follow, a decision that may be based on the prevailing weather. On fine days walking on the downs is an exhilarating experience, but wind and rain can so often spoil the party. In such conditions the exposed hills can be an uncomfortable place, and most of us prefer to stay at home. But it took more than a mere drop of rain to deter Charles Sorley from his regular walks. Indeed he even relished the prospect of a good soaking, so that he could return to college and record the experience in verse:

> And here we strove, and here we felt each vein
> Ice-bound, each limb fast frozen, all night long.
> And here we held communion with the rain
> That lashed us into manhood with its thong,
> Cleansing through pain.
> And the wind visited us and made us strong.

3 If you prefer to follow the shorter route, take the first turning on your left as you reach the signpost. Proceed along a similar track, which is rutted and likely to be muddy. After 800m a farmhouse comes into view in the distance, just before we reach a junction in the trees. Here we leave the main track, which continues ahead. Turn right, then immediately left, as indicated by the byway and Three Downs Link arrows on the gate post. Do not go through the gate. After a further 200m is Bytham Farm. Cross the road and continue straight on past the house and farm buildings, to eventually join up with both the Ridgeway and our longer route at point 5 (SU 211738).

4 The longer route from the signpost forks left along the tarmac road between the farm buildings. Just beyond them is a byway crossing where our route is signed straight on as Byway to Whiteshard Bottom. From this point we follow it for 1.25 miles (2 km) on a mixture of tarmac and hard track, finally descending beside trees to a junction (SU 226733). Turn sharp left, almost 180 degrees, signed as Byway to Ridgeway. This is a stony chalk track that climbs gradually beside trees, and past Blue Barn, to meet the Ridgeway at a byway crossing (SU 211738). The shorter route joins from our left, and there are signs here warning about prohibited vehicle access. Turn right.

5 Both routes now follow the Ridgeway northwards for 700m to the next junction, which is a staggered crossing (SU 214744). Turn left onto a narrow byway, with views across to the Ogbourne Downs golf course. The descent is not steep, and after joining up with another byway we continue on tarmac past some industrial buildings. Cross the minor road, and turn left onto the Chiseldon – Marlborough railway path (SU 204740).

An icy morning on Poulton Downs

We have now reached the trackbed of the old Marlborough – Swindon railway line, as well as the course of the Wanborough–Mildenhall Roman road. Passing Ogbourne St George, both of these former highways have now been overlaid by the A346. The dead straight alignment of the present-day road is a clear indication that it replaces the Roman road all the way to Chiseldon. Over the same stretch, the railway trackbed runs parallel, and is now part of National Cycle route No 45. The Roman road continues south to Mildenhall, once a major settlement called *Cunetio*, where more than 50,000 Roman coins were unearthed in 1978. The railway curves away and, like the modern road, follows the course of the River Og into Marlborough.

MIDLAND & SOUTH WESTERN JUNCTION RAILWAY. After the main railways from London to Bristol and the West of England had been completed, Marlborough found itself isolated with no access to the network. This, and the rapid decline of the stagecoach business, caused numerous problems for students at the college. As a result the bursar campaigned for a branch line to connect the town to the main line at Savernake Junction, which subsequently opened in 1864. Attempts to extend the line, both south to Andover, and northwards to Swindon, began in 1872. Nine years later the first trains ran on the northern extension, with intermediate stations at Chiseldon and Ogbourne. Early financial problems forced the newly formed Swindon, Marlborough & Andover Railway to seek other partners interested in creating a through route to link the Midlands with the south coast. It was an idea that had already been put forward several times, but failed due to overwhelming opposition from the Great Western Railway, which dominated the region. Despite this, the proposal went ahead, and in 1884 the Midland & South Western Junction Railway was formed. However, it was not until the turn of the century that numerous operating problems were finally resolved. One of these was to build a new line from Marlborough to Savernake Junction, taking a more direct route through a tunnel that survives today as a bat sanctuary. Until its entrance was sealed, boys from the nearby college would often sneak into its darkness for secret smoking of home-rolled cigarettes! The arrival of the army on Salisbury Plain helped to boost the railway's revenue, as did the increase in military traffic during two world wars. Regular consignments of milk were also carried, with up to 12,000 gallons a day despatched to London from stations between Cricklade and Andover. However, amalgamation of the country's railways in 1923 effectively handed the M&SWJR to the Great Western. As a result, decline had already started long before the widespread closures of the 1960s. The last college train ran in 1964, after which the track was lifted, and a century of Marlborough's railways came to an end. Although some sections have since been incorporated into the surrounding landscape, much of the line can still be traced. As well as the cycle path between Chiseldon and Marlborough, a further length of trackbed across Swindon is retained for cyclists and pedestrians, while at Broad Blunsdon, a stretch of line is being restored.

6 Follow the railway path all the way back to point 2. Just before the junction we crossed earlier, turn right to re-cross the A346, and retrace your steps through the village to the layby at Bay Bridge.

CHARLES HAMILTON SORLEY (1895-1915). Born in Aberdeen, Charles Sorley came from a literary background. His father and grandfather had written several books between them, and his mother read Shakespeare to her three children. Five years later, the family moved to Cambridge, where Charles attended Kings College Choir School. He excelled in English, and at the age of 13, won a scholarship to Marlborough College. It was the start of a love affair with the Wiltshire Downs. He enjoyed the solitary pursuits of running and walking, often roaming far and wide, gathering his thoughts for some inspirational poetry. Such was his love of the countryside that he would cut short his train ride back to Cambridge, and walk some of the way instead. On one occasion in 1912 he even walked the entire journey – a four day trip of 100 miles. Having gained a place at University College, Oxford, he quit his last term at Marlborough to study in Germany. But his timing was unfortunate, and as war broke out in 1914 he found himself an enemy alien, and was briefly imprisoned as a spy until his credentials could be verified. Arriving home, he made the difficult decision to enlist, and initial training on the Berkshire Downs brought back memories of the hills around Marlborough that feature many times in his poems. Now his poetry changed course. With strong reservations about the war, his words began to challenge the morality of conflict, even creating an apocalyptic vision of humanity:

> And nations, ankle-deep in love and hate,
> Throw darts and kisses all the unwitting hour
> Beside the ominous unseen tide of fate;
> And there is emptiness and drink and power.

As the conflict intensified, his unit was ordered to France. Together with so many others, he never saw Britain again, his short life ended by a sniper's bullet. Written only days earlier, his final poem, and possibly his best, was discovered in his kit bag:

> When you see millions of the mouthless dead
> Across your dreams in pale battalions go,
> Say not soft things as other men have said,
> That you'll remember. For you need not so . . .

> . . . Then, scanning all the o'ercrowded mass, should you
> Perceive one face that you loved heretofore,
> It is a spook. None wears the face you knew.
> Great death has made all his for evermore.

Further reading:

Sorley, Charles Hamilton, 1916, *Marlborough and other poems.* (Cambridge University Press)

Wilson, Jean Moorcroft, 1985, *Charles Hamilton Sorley – a biography.* (Cecil Woolf)

Wilson, Jean Moorcroft, 1985, *The Collected Poems of Charles Hamilton Sorley.* (Cecil Woolf)

5 Highways and Byways
Bishopstone and the Hinton Downs
(7.25 miles/11.6 km) or (6.25 miles/10 km)
(OS Explorers 157 & 170)

Much has been written of travel, far less of the road.(Edward Thomas)

By its very nature, the Ridgeway crosses high ground that is constantly exposed to the elements, with little shelter when the weather deteriorates. The same can be said of the adjacent downland that makes up the greater part of this walk. Choose the right day, however, and you will be rewarded with views that extend not only across this north-east corner of Wiltshire, but well beyond into neighbouring Oxfordshire. Situated less than a mile (1.6 km) from the county boundary, the village of Bishopstone has all the necessary ingredients that combine to create a delightful community – white-washed thatched cottages, a winding stream, mill pond, church and pubs. Our route detours from the Ridgeway to pass through the village on another ancient road, before returning to the open downs for a high level stroll to the motorway and back. The gradients are moderately steep, but fairly lengthy in places. Muddy conditions are inevitable after recent rain, although the Ridgeway section here is much improved of late. Refreshments are available at the Royal Oak and the True Heart in Bishopstone, both clearly signed in the village, as well as the Shepherds Rest at Foxhill crossroads, where the walk begins. Originally known as Totterdown, this was once the meeting place of the Ridgeway and Ermin Street, which we shall encounter as we progress.

Alfred Williams knew this area well, and writing in the early 20th century he provided us with a colourful description of the countryside in his book Villages of the White Horse:

> There could be nothing more tenderly sweet and soothing than the
> view of Charlbury Hill and the Bishopstone and Ashbury slopes from

the top of the road that brings you up from Wanborough to the Shepherds Rest. The still, calm beauty, the charming interfusion of colour, the soft radiance of light – especially in the afternoon – and the overpowering sense of rest, hold you spellbound; you seem to melt and dissolve into it, to feel the beautiful within you, and when you go forward through the fresh, pure air, you are like another being, a thing new created.

---

1 **Park alongside the Bishopstone road, about 100m from Foxhill crossroads (SU 232814). Walk up the road to a large Ridgeway sign, and turn right along the rough tarmac track. As you progress, Charlbury Hill is passed on your left, its isolated 253m summit topped by a concrete trig pillar. Just beyond it the Ridgeway starts a long descent. Part of the way down is a gate and two stiles on the left. The second stile displays a Countryside Stewardship waymarker. (SU 243821).**

COUNTRYSIDE STEWARDSHIP SCHEME. This government initiative was established in 1991 to extend the footpath network in areas where public access was limited, often linking fragmented paths to create a circular route. In some cases this may open up an area of land where the public can roam freely, while elsewhere pedestrians are able to use permissive paths for a specific period of time. Typically this might be 10 years, at the end of which permission can be either withdrawn or extended. In return, landowners derive certain financial benefits. Due to their temporary nature, permissive paths are not shown on Ordnance Survey maps. Details of those paths established by the CSS can be found on the internet at www.countrywalks.defra.gov.uk. Individual maps are usually displayed alongside each path, often fixed to a fence or post. Otherwise look for green and white arrows. Currently there are about 60 approved sites across Wiltshire, and one of them allows us to visit an exceptionally well preserved ancient field system.

2 Cross the second stile, and follow the fence along the field edge to another stile at the far end, overlooking an enclosed coombe. Veer right to descend into and along the valley floor, with raised farming terraces on either side.

STRIP LYNCHETS. In Britain today we take food supplies for granted. Centuries ago it was an entirely different matter. Most families had to be self-sufficient, and if bad weather caused a poor harvest many went hungry. Across the country different farming methods were employed to use the land efficiently. One was to create long parallel terraces along the contours of steep hillsides, rather like a wide staircase. The hillsides were ploughed horizontally, thus forcing the earth to creep downhill until it encountered an obstruction. Chalk slopes were popular as the light cohesive soil easily formed the banks, but the downside was their inability to retain the required level of fertility. Consequently, many were soon abandoned in favour of sheep grazing, and it is in these areas that strip lynchets have survived in greatest numbers. Sometimes called lynches or shepherds steps, many are difficult to date. One common theory was to link them to the desperate need for extra farmland during the 12th and 13th centuries, when the population was growing rapidly. Most probably evolved during that period, although evidence exists to indicate a much earlier date in some cases. Excavated lynchets in Cornwall and Dorset have yielded artefacts from the Bronze Age, and pre-Roman pottery was discovered in a

The strip lynchets at Bishopstone are some of the best in the country

lynchet near Winchester. Several sites can be found throughout Wiltshire, but undoubtedly the best is at Bishopstone. At certain times of the year the low angle of the sun dramatically highlights the terraces, but you will not see them from the Ridgeway, as they are hidden from passing traffic. This may have been a deliberate ploy by our ancestors, who wished to guard their precious crops from unscrupulous travellers.

3 As you proceed along the valley floor, aim for the distant white houses, and exit the field over a stile beside two gates (SU 245830). To bypass the village of Bishopstone, and reduce the walk by one mile (1.6 km), turn right along the valley floor and continue from point 5. Otherwise walk ahead to the second double gateway, and go through the kissing gate on the right. Leave the next field by another kissing gate, leading to a hillside path that emerges between two staddle stones onto a track by a thatched cottage. Walk along the gravel drive to exit onto a minor road, and continue along the main village road, which carries the name Icknield Way.

THE ICKNIELD WAY. Just like the Ridgeway, this is another prehistoric trade route. Although we cannot date it with any certainty, some believe it to be as old as the Ridgeway, and may even be the same road. Indeed for much of its length it seems to run parallel to the Ridgeway, but at a slightly lower level. This raises speculation that it was simply an alternative route. Little evidence remains, yet Edward Thomas managed to devote an entire book to this ancient route, which he walked from Norfolk to Wiltshire in 1911. The name Icknield is mysterious. Some associate it with the Iceni people who once lived in East Anglia, yet it re-appears as various different spellings in other parts of England and Wales. Edward Thomas may well have been correct when he concluded that it was simply an old name for a road. Today Icknield Way is the name given to a long distance footpath that extends from Norfolk to Ivinghoe Beacon in Buckinghamshire, where it meets the Ridgeway. Together with the Peddars Way and the Wessex Ridgeway, these four trails combine to form a 363-mile (583 km) route from Lyme Regis in Dorset to Hunstanton on the Norfolk coast – collectively known as the Great Ridgeway.

The village pond in Bishopstone

4 Follow the village road around to the left to go past the pond. Continue along the pavement on the other side as far as Prebendal Farm. Before the bend, cross back over the road to a bridleway sign opposite, pointing to the Ridgeway. Follow this track out of the village to the double gates passed earlier (SU 245830). Cross over the outward route by forking left along the enclosed valley.

5 At the far end, go through the gate and turn right. Climb up through the narrow gorge on either track, aiming for a gate and signpost on the Ridgeway (SU 249823). Briefly turn left onto the Ridgeway, then immediately right onto a signed bridleway. This is a wide rutted track in a bare open landscape. Follow it for two miles (3.2 km) to a minor road on Peaks Down (SU 260795). On the way you pass an isolated farmhouse, where a map on a post describes another area of land, adjacent to the bridleway, set aside under the Countryside Stewardship Scheme. From here the track surface improves.

The minor road here is roughly the route of the Thieves Way, a medieval track used by drovers. Judging by its name, the cattle may well have been stolen. At this location the Thieves Way crossed Ermin Street, built by the Romans to connect Cirencester to Silchester. Nowadays the Roman road is overlaid by the A419 dual carriageway as far as Wanborough, then by the minor road through Foxhill crossroads to Baydon. Although predominantly straight, it curves slightly on Peaks Down, where the two roads met. Neither is visible today, but you cannot fail to notice the much more recent highway beneath which both are now buried. The sound of traffic on the M4 motorway has gradually intensified as we crossed the Hinton Downs. Having left our oldest road earlier, we now encounter one of our newest – a time span of more than 5,000 years. The volume of traffic has increased somewhat during that period! Comparing the M4 and the Ridgeway in his book *Chalkways of South and South-East England*, Edward C Pyatt writes: "No greater incongruity can be imagined than the juxtaposition of these roads ancient and modern".

6 Turn right along the minor road to reach the motorway bridge, but do not cross over. Immediately before it, turn right onto a signed bridleway, then bear right again at another sign. Pass a large storage tank, then turn left onto a wide grass track, parallel to gallops on your left. Follow this track, almost dead straight, for two miles (3.2 km) back to the Ridgeway (SU 235816).

During this section of our walk we climb to our highest point at 245m as we pass a circular reservoir. The Foxhill transmitter is ahead, while directly behind, but further away, is the tall slender mast at Membury Services on the M4. Over to the east the outline of White Horse Hill has been visible for some time, across the Oxfordshire border at Uffington. On the opposite horizon is Liddington Hill.

Author H W Timperley (1890-1961) fell in love with Wiltshire during his Territorial Army training on Salisbury Plain. He returned to write *Ridge Way Country*, and was so fascinated with the area around Bishopstone that he subsequently went to live there in a delightful cottage by the stream. His enthusiasm for "the silvery quality of the air and the quiet undulations of the land" clearly shows throughout his book:

> By a freeing and enlarging peacefulness, the downland scene takes the mind far from the influence of irritating, noisy, and belittling distractions... [he wrote in 1935] ...then, when it is at one with itself and with the country-side, a new strength seems to flow into it, sour emotions are purified, twisted thoughts are made straight, the whole being responds to the large rhythms of the land and its airy sky, and the mind, whatever its burdens, becomes buoyant with new power.

7 To return to Foxhill crossroads, turn left at the barn and retrace your steps along the Ridgeway.

EDWARD THOMAS (1878-1917). Although born in London of Welsh parents, Edward Thomas spent much of his short adult life in Wiltshire, which he regarded as his favourite county. After graduating from Oxford in 1901, he embarked on a literary career that involved long periods travelling around southern England. Several books followed, largely based on his own experiences. Like many others of his profession, he found peace and inspiration in the natural beauty of the countryside, and his books provide a unique record of the English landscape of a century ago. Always anxious to find the truth, he was never prepared to compromise on the facts. Although he strove hard for success, he was never totally satisfied with his efforts. At one point he turned down the chance to write a guide to Wiltshire, which would undoubtedly have become a county classic today. Only towards the end of his life did he discover the impulse to write poetry, and it was here that he found the satisfaction that had previously eluded him, and for which he has since achieved the widest recognition. When war began in 1914 he enlisted, even though he was not required to do so. At first he spent his army life on home soil, but shortly after embarkation to France, he lost his life at Arras. Although his poems were not directly aimed at the war, his words hint at the suffering and heartbreak of conflict in foreign lands.

> The flowers left thick at nightfall in the wood
> This Eastertide call into mind the men,
> Now far from home, who, with their sweethearts, should
> Have gathered them and will do never again.

Further reading:

Thomas, Edward, 1980, *The Icknield Way*. (Wildwood House)
Thomas, Edward, 1981, *In Pursuit of Spring*. (Wildwood House)
Timperley, H W, 1935, *Ridge Way Country*. (J M Dent)
Williams, Alfred, 2007, *Villages of the White Horse*. (Nonsuch Publishing)

6 **Riverside ramblings**

Littlecote House and Ramsbury

(7.25 miles /11.6 km) or (6 miles/9.6 km)

(OS Explorers 157 & 158)

This walk explores the tranquil Kennet valley, where Romans once lived and built an impressive villa. A short distance away a more recent mansion still stands, its long history dominated by a particularly gruesome event. Elsewhere, we shall discover a building connection of a different sort that called for a local election to decide the fate of an old tree.

With a choice of routes available, we follow bridleways, fieldpaths, and one or two minor roads, never far from the river that gave this valley its name. Although we avoid the floodplain as far as possible, it is worth remembering that in very wet conditions the river spills over into surrounding fields, when some sections of our route will be waterlogged or may even be impassable. There is one steep climb, but other gradients are minor. Refreshments can be found in Ramsbury and Chilton Foliat.

1 Park in the layby on the B4192 at the western end of Chilton Foliat (SU 317705). Walk back towards the speed limit signs and turn right at the Littlecote signpost. Follow the path through the woodland, cross over the river, and emerge onto a minor road.

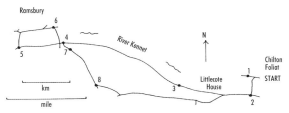

In summer the woodland floor is a colourful profusion of wildflowers that thrive in the damp, shaded conditions. As I walked along here early one morning the birds were singing happily in the trees, while at the river a heron took to the air. Nesting peacefully on the far bank, a family of mute swans was less concerned by my presence, although the adults kept a close watch over their young offspring until I was well out of the way.

2 Turn right along the minor road until you reach the East Lodge entrance to Littlecote Park (SU 311702), where a sign advertises Warners Hotels. Go through the main gate and follow the drive up to, and past, the house.

Viewed from either side, Littlecote House is impressive, and its gardens have featured in *Country Life* magazine several times. On the north side colourful herbaceous borders surround neatly mown lawns, while to the south a large grass area has been set aside for wildflowers.

Littlecote House

First mentioned in Domesday Book, the Manor of Littlecote was occupied by the Durnford family until about 1290, when it passed to the de Calstones. Then in 1415 the heiress, Elizabeth de Calstone married William Darrell, whose ancestors arrived in Britain during the Norman Conquest. Darrell, a key figure in Richard II's government, therefore acquired the estate. The royal connection continued through their son, George, and his son, Edward, who was vice-chancellor to Catherine of Aragon, first wife of Henry VIII. The king himself visited Littlecote in 1520, and subsequently returned a few years later to court Jane Seymour, whose family lived nearby. It was during this period that the present day mansion began to take shape. In 1531 the death of Sir Edward Darrell allowed his grandson, also

The Great Hall at Littlecote House

Sir Edward, to inherit the estate. His extravagant lifestyle crippled the family finances, resulting in a bequest that left the manor to his mistress, rather than his widow. William, his son, followed in his father's reckless footsteps. Scandal, bribery, fraud and debauchery were regular events in his cavalier attitude to life. As well as falling out with most of his neighbours, he was even imprisoned twice for slandering the queen. But one of his crimes stands out, and has provided a topic for debate ever since.

Various accounts have been published about the events of one dark night in November 1575. The facts may vary, but they all lead to one sinister conclusion. Mrs Barnes, a midwife from nearby Shefford, was awoken by a stranger who offered her a handsome fee if she would attend to a nobleman's lady about to give birth. She agreed, but had to be blindfolded until she arrived at the patient's bedside. A man was also present, but both he and the expectant mother were disguised. On delivering the baby boy, the man ordered the midwife to throw him on the open fire in the adjacent room. Horrified, she refused, whereupon the man snatched the baby from her and carried out the awful deed himself. Later the midwife was taken home, again blindfolded, but not before she had taken the precaution of cutting a piece of cloth from the bedroom, and counting the number of stairs leading to it. Armed with this evidence, she reported the matter to the local magistrate, who instigated a search that led them to Littlecote House. 'Wild' Darrell, as he had become known, was identified as the culprit, and stood trial for murder. Somehow he was acquitted, apparently due to the intervention of his cousin, Sir John

Popham, a senior lawyer. Darrell escaped justice to resume his reckless lifestyle, but while galloping at full speed through the estate in 1589, his horse reared up and threw him to the ground, breaking his neck. Legend claims the horse had been spooked by the ghost of the murdered child. As a reward for his services, Sir John Popham inherited the Littlecote estate, and it remained in his family for 340 years, during which time royalty and other important guests were frequently entertained.

In the Civil War one of the medieval halls was converted into a Cromwellian chapel, distinguished by the position of its pulpit in place of the altar. Today it survives as the only example of its kind. Among the many other rooms that display features from past eras is the great hall, where a collection of civil war armaments is displayed above an oak shuffleboard table, and the long gallery, designed for indoor exercise during bad weather. And just along the corridor is the bedroom where Wild Darrell murdered his son. A fire no longer burns in the grate, but the spirit of the newborn infant refuses to leave. The ghost of his mother has also been seen wandering the old house in search of her lost child. Since 1997, guests of Warners Hotels have been able to occupy rooms close to the haunted bedroom. Some feel uneasy as they make their way back to their rooms along the quiet, dimly-lit corridors late at night!

The unique Cromwellian chapel in Littlecote House is clearly identified by its pulpit instead of an altar

3 After passing the house, continue straight on to a crosstracks, and take a detour to the right to inspect the site of the Roman villa and its mosaic.

THE ORPHEUS MOSAIC. Archaeological discoveries have identified human activity around here as far back as 20,000 BC, but it was the Romans who created a lasting impression. Early in their occupation of Britain they built a military road through the Kennet valley to supply troops advancing westwards. The river here would have been shallow enough to become an important crossing point, so a settlement soon developed. Together with other buildings a two storey villa was constructed, complete with kitchen, bathroom, and underfloor heating. Around 360 AD, a flint barn was converted into a religious or ceremonial hall. Inside, a vast mosaic floor was laid, illuminated by shafts of light through windows in the roof. The centre of the mosaic featured an engraving of Orpheus, the mythological priest of Apollo, surrounded by representations of the four seasons. Half a century later the Roman occupation ended; decay set in, the villa was demolished, and the mosaic buried. It did not see the light of day again for another 12 centuries, and even then only briefly. When the estate steward uncovered part of the mosaic in 1727, Sir Francis Popham ordered it to be reburied, as he feared it would attract unwanted publicity. A further 250 years passed before it was rediscovered by an archaeologist in 1976, together with the foundations of the adjacent villa. Since then the mosaic has been restored, and this unique site is now protected from further damage.

4 Leave the villa site by continuing along the same track, never far from the river. Go past the rounded wall of West Lodge, and stay on the track all the way to Ambrose Farm (SU 279713). To exclude Ramsbury, turn left at the bridleway signpost just before the farm, and continue from point 7. Otherwise, proceed to the road, and cross over, signed Mill Lane.

5 Follow Mill Lane as far as two thatched cottages (SU 270712), and turn right between them to cross the river on two footbridges. Emerging onto the High Street, turn right and follow it to the Bell Inn.

In front of the public house is a tree; but not just any old tree. In fact it's a relatively new tree, yet its story begins in 1846 when the Provident Union and Investment Society was founded here. Later to become the Ramsbury Building Society, it adopted as its symbol the elm tree that had stood outside the Bell Inn for over 300 years. Like many of the elms at Littlecote, the tree died of disease, and for some time locals argued over its fate. Many wanted to replace it, while others warned that its removal would invoke a witch's curse. Eventually a village referendum was held, and by a small majority the decision to replace it was upheld. Consequently in 1986, the national media descended on Ramsbury to witness the planting of the present tree – an English oak from Epping Forest.

6 Fork right of the Bell Inn as far as The Knap, and turn right along the Froxfield road to return to Ambrose Farm (SU 279713). Turn left, then at the bridleway signpost passed earlier, fork right to rejoin the shorter route.

7 At first the gradient is gentle, but approaching Whitehill Coppice it becomes progressively steeper. In wet conditions be careful of the exposed chalk, which can be slippery. At an intersection in the trees, ignore the first track on the right, and just beyond it fork right at the second. The gradient eases beside an open field on our right. Emerging at a bend on a concrete road, continue ahead, descending to the valley bottom (SU 285704).

8 Turn left at the 3-way signpost, still on a rough concrete track. At the next junction turn left of the signpost (SU 290701). Stay on this track for almost a mile (1.6 km) to pass Littlecote House, and continue along the tarmac road. Emerging between pillars, continue straight on down the road to pass the East Lodge, and retrace your steps back to Chilton Foliat.

Littlecote House and gardens are open to the public for various events and activities. For details telephone 01488 682509.

Further reading:

Warner, 1997, *Littlecote - A History*. (Warner Holidays Ltd)
Croucher, Barbara, 1986, *The Village in the Valley; a history of Ramsbury*
Croucher, Barbara, 1995, *Ramsbury then and now*. (Privately published)

7 Kennet Country
Axford and Ramsbury

(6.75 miles/10.8 km) or (5 miles/8 km)

(OS Explorer 157)

Having sampled the delights of the Kennet valley in our previous walk, it is appropriate that we should continue our journey along the river as it meanders gently through the peaceful countryside further upstream. From Axford we follow the floodplain to Ramsbury, where we shall learn more of the village history. Then our return route climbs moderate gradients to reach the site of an old wartime airfield, offering extensive views to the distant Inkpen Hill escarpment where Wiltshire, Berkshire and Hampshire meet. Further on, the view is across the Kennet valley, as we drop down to cross the floodplain once again.

1 Start in Axford, where a small, roughly surfaced car park can be found a short distance along the road from the Red Lion pub (SU 240702). Turn right out of the car park, and follow the road almost to the speed limit signs. Alongside Ivy Cottage go through the gate onto a signposted path, parallel to the road. Continue through the trees to emerge into a field beside the river (SU 246704).

Over the centuries, Axford had two manor houses, one in the village, and the other at Axford Farm, where the remains of an old chapel have been discovered. Older versions of the Explorer map for this area show the footpath going right past the farm, but this is no longer correct. The present route avoids the farm altogether by turning south near Cowleaze Cottages to cross the three main river channels on footbridges, before rejoining the original route at a bridleway junction. Fortunately the way is clearly marked and easy to follow, with signs to guide you where appropriate. The floodplain is quite wide here, and can be waterlogged at times.

2 Follow the riverbank to the first footbridge, and cross over. Continue across the floodplain and two more river channels, then immediately turn left as instructed (SU 248700). Proceed along the riverbank to merge with a bridleway at a junction, and follow it straight ahead for 1200m to a group of houses by speed ramp signs (SU 262709). Remember this location for later in the walk.

Footbridge over one of the channels in the Kennet floodplain

On our left-hand side is Ramsbury Manor Park, and through the trees we can see the splendid brick mansion built in 1681 by Sir William Jones, a prosperous lawyer, shortly after he had acquired the estate. His relatives, the Burdett family, succeeded him, and in 1775 the park and grounds were re-modelled to include an ornamental lake. More recent owners have included Baron Rootes, the motor manufacturer, and property tycoon Harry Hyams, who in 2006 was the victim of one of the country's largest burglaries, when high quality works of art were stolen.

Long before all this, the manor was owned by the Bishop of Ramsbury, a position that was established in 909 AD when the existing dioceses of Winchester and Sherborne were sub-divided into a number of smaller ministries. Ramsbury was chosen as the seat of the diocese of Wiltshire and Berkshire, with Athelstan as its first bishop. His successor, Odo, went on to become Archbishop of Canterbury in 942 AD. So did Sigeric, who came to Ramsbury from Glastonbury. Another bishop,

Aelfric, should have followed in their footsteps, but his election was never ratified by the monarch. On his death in 1005, he bequeathed a ship to the people of Wiltshire, an unusual gift to a land-locked county. Despite its relatively small size, Ramsbury was clearly regarded as an important episcopal centre, but it was never really large enough to withstand the changes that occurred after the Norman Conquest. Consequently, the bishopric was transferred to Old Sarum in 1075, and thereafter the title lay dormant until 1974, when the 11th bishop was installed. The original Saxon cathedral eventually disappeared, and in its place the present Holy Cross church now stands.

3 Bear left along the tarmac drive, cross two bridges at the end of the lake, and emerge on the road by the entrance gates. To follow the shorter route, cross the road at the bend, and bear right onto the footpath in front of you, which runs parallel to the road into Ramsbury. Entering the village by Hilldrop Lane, continue to the start of Back Lane, where you rejoin the long route at point 6, (SU 270715) and turn right.

4 Otherwise, to follow the long route from the entrance gates, cross the road and fork left along the pavement as far as Manor Farm (SU 261715). Just after the farmhouse, bear right onto a signposted bridleway. Approaching Staghorn Copse the chalk track climbs fairly steeply, then levels off before emerging onto Hilldrop Lane

beside a farm. Cross the road, signed as byway to Aldbourne, follow the main track around left, then downhill to a crosstracks (SU 263727).

5 Turn right through the gateway and along the field edge. Go through another gate into the next field, and bear right along the bottom edge. Exit in the far corner by a gate and stile. Follow the wire fence beside the wood, and past a farm on a

Ramsbury Manor and lake

40

gravel drive. Where the gravel bends to the right, proceed ahead to exit onto the road by the signpost. Turn left along Knowledge Hill. At the end continue on the pavement beside garage No 12. Fork right on an enclosed path. Emerge on Back Lane, turn right and follow it to the end. Rejoin the short route where the main road enters the village at a bend (SU 270715). Turn left.

Although of lesser importance today, the road through Ramsbury was once part of the main highway from London to Bath and Bristol. From Hungerford, where it was called the Plow Way, the old road passed through Ramsbury along Back Lane, as the lower High Street was prone to regular flooding from the river in those days. From here it followed the river to Axford, but when the manor park was extended in 1775, it had to be diverted over White's Hill. This became a notoriously difficult route, with coaches often losing control and overturning on the steep gradient. By this time, however, an easier route had been established through Savernake Forest, but being part of the turnpike system it demanded toll charges from those using it. Inevitably, some travellers continued to follow the original road, including drovers, thus adding to its deterioration, and prompting one publication of the day to describe it as "a miserable wagon track".

RAMSBURY. Evidence shows that Bronze Age people visited the Kennet valley, but did not settle. Later the Romans also found it to their liking, building a villa at Littlecote and a garrison town at Mildenhall (Cunetio). However, Ramsbury itself was largely ignored due to its isolated location, bypassed by three Roman roads. It was left to the Saxons to create the first village community here in the 7th century, when they called it *Hraefnburg*, meaning a raven's fort. They were responsible for introducing iron smelting and farming, although it was the spread of Christianity that really put Ramsbury on the map.

Over the next few centuries, various trades developed, including cloth, candle-making, milling, and brewing. Ramsbury beer was highly rated, thanks to the river water, which was both plentiful and of good quality. It also came in useful when fires broke out – a regular event in past times. In 1648 a disastrous blaze destroyed 130 properties, and another in 1781 struck 40 more, plus several outbuildings and a malthouse. Then in 1862 another 25 cottages went up in smoke. Consequently, few timber and thatch properties survive in the centre of the village. By the end of the 18th century the brewing industry was thriving, with regular exports to London. But as the Industrial Revolution progressed, Ramsbury found itself bypassed once again, this time by the railways. Rival breweries with better transport links were able to offer a quicker service by rail, and hence Ramsbury's brewing industry steadily declined. However, in 2004 this local tradition was revived, and Ramsbury ales can once again be found at several outlets in the area.

Farming was also affected by the widespread changes of the 19th century. Angered by economic distress, enforced mechanisation, and a succession of harsh winters, destitute farm labourers across southern England attacked landowners and wrecked agricultural equipment. Several local people were among more than 8,000 that were arrested and transported. Ring-leaders were executed. Others found alternative employment at the new railway works in Swindon, while some emigrated to South America to rear sheep.

6 Follow the main road the short distance to the first bend where the High Street goes left to the centre of the village. Bear right into Mill Lane, and cross two river channels (SU 270713). In front of the thatched cottages, veer right to go through a gate on a bridleway. Where the track divides, take the left-hand option. Stay on this track/ tarmac until you reach the houses passed earlier in point 2 (SU 262709).

7 After the last house, bear left on a wide fence-lined track that climbs past a thatched cottage and into the trees. The gradient then increases and we take the middle track at a 3-way intersection, to continue all the way to Park Farm (SU 255698).

RAMSBURY AIRFIELD. As we climb up to Park Farm, the hilltop on our left was once an airfield, constructed in 1941 as a training base for the RAF. Three concrete runways were laid, each built to bomber standards. Living accommodation was provided for 2,400 personnel, and when completed the 500-acre site became part of No 92 Group, Bomber Command.

Within days of its opening, American troops arrived with Dakota C-47 aircraft, but shortly afterwards departed for North Africa. Training continued throughout 1943, resulting in several accidents in the locality. After the war ended the airfield briefly continued its role as a training base, but closure soon followed and the last recorded military aircraft to use Ramsbury was a Spitfire that made an emergency landing in 1947. For a while the site was used for temporary accommodation, until the post-war housing crisis eased. Thereafter, agriculture returned, with parts of the old runways being retained as farm roads.

8 Arriving at Park Farm, turn right beside the Three Downs Link waymarkers, to follow the yellow arrow through the tree plantation. Cross the stile on the far side, and fork left along the top of the field. At the end ignore the first gate. Instead, look right of it to locate a yellow arrow on a post, leading to a second gate. Cross the track (SU 250698) to continue downhill beside the fence. Then fork left to follow the direction of the overhead cables, and exit onto a fence-lined bridleway. Fork left along it for 150m, to a stile with yellow arrow on your right. Cross the field diagonally to the house (SU 242699). Veer right in front of it, and along the wide footpath. Cross the river and floodplain to exit onto the road in Axford. Turn left back to the car park.

RIVER KENNET. '...the Kennet urged its peaceful course through lush meadows and straggling osier beds, so close at hand that you could hear the moorhens, splashing and uttering their harsh cries in the tall reeds.'

So wrote A G Bradley about the largest tributary of the Thames. As one of our finest chalk streams, much of the upper Kennet is designated as a Site of Special Scientific Interest to protect its rich variety of plant species and wildlife. The Stream Water Crowfoot is one of the few species of water weed able to thrive in the main current of a fast flowing river. Its presence here is a sign of the excellent quality of the water. Other indicators can be found swimming below the surface, in particular brown trout. Writing in 1907, A G Bradley claims that '. . . the

The return journey to Axford provides extensive views across the Kennet valley

three largest river trout ever taken in England, came out of the Kennet . . .'

The meadows on either side of the river are home to numerous birds. It is even said that nightingales return each year from Africa to sing from the same bush. As well as ducks, herons and the occasional kingfisher, the river is also a regular haunt of the water vole, whose numbers have declined by around 90% during the past 40 years, due largely to loss of habitat, pollution, and the release of mink into the wild. The clear, unpolluted water of the Kennet is ideal for this much loved creature, who found fame as 'Ratty' in *The Wind in the Willows*. As you walk along the riverbank, listen for the characteristic 'plop' – the tell-tale sign that a water vole is nearby.

Further reading:

Day, Roger, 2004, *Ramsbury at War: a Wiltshire village and its airfield 1939-1945*. (Privately published)

Bradley, A G, 1907, *Round About Wiltshire*. (Methuen)

8 Out in a Cold Snap
Aldbourne and Two Deserted Villages

(7.75 miles/12.4 km) or (5.5 miles/8.8 km)

(OS Explorer 157)

Winter on the Downs can be bitter, especially when a chilling wind is blowing from the north or east. But on a calm day, when the sun is shining and the ground is frozen hard, it can be a different place altogether. Early in the morning, after a sharp hoar frost has coated everything in delicate white crystals, or a light dusting of snow highlights and accentuates the natural contours of the landscape, even the deep trenches of a rutted track can look enchanting. Venture out onto the hills on days like this and you will be richly rewarded. However, such conditions are rare, and short-lived. The recent succession of mild, wet winters has provided few opportunities for walking in the snow, and when they do occur you have to be quick to take advantage before they disappear. One such occasion was just after Christmas a few years ago. Although I cannot promise the same glorious weather, join me on a downland walk to the highest village in the county, and past the site of another that was deserted in controversial circumstances. The views are stunning, but the climb up to them is not too severe, mostly long and gradual. Some of the tracks are deeply rutted and likely to be muddy or waterlogged at times. Parking is available in the centre of Aldbourne, with pubs nearby.

1 Start at the pond in the centre of Aldbourne (SU 265756). Leave the village by walking along the left-hand side of the B4192 towards Swindon, initially on pavement then along the grass verge. After 1200m we reach a signposted byway opposite New Barn (SU 255762).

Several Wiltshire villages lay claim to the origins of the Moonraker legend, but Aldbourne's pond has a different tale to tell. Long ago a strange bird was seen swimming in the pond. Nobody could identify it, until the oldest inhabitant declared it to be a dabchick, otherwise known as the Little Grebe. Since then residents of Aldbourne have been nicknamed Dabchicks, and today are proud of the fact, adopting it as the name of their parish magazine.

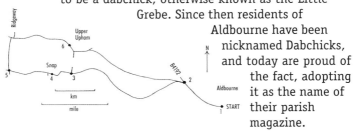

MOONRAKERS. Smuggling is not normally associated with land-locked Wiltshire, but the forests that once covered the county more than they do today, were ideal hiding places for contraband brought up from the coast. So it was not uncommon to see customs officers patrolling the country lanes. One moonlit night two excisemen stumbled across a pair of locals who seemed to be raking the surface of the village pond. When questioned, the locals jovially explained that they were trying to retrieve their cheese. Examining the pond more closely, the excisemen realised that the 'cheese' was merely the moon's reflection on the water. They concluded that the locals were just a pair of half-wits, and went on their way, laughing. But it was the locals who had the last laugh, for as soon as the officers were out of sight, they raked in the real cheese – kegs of illegal brandy hidden at the bottom of the pond. The story has been told many times since, and Wiltshire people became known as Moonrakers.

2 Turn left along the wide byway, then fork left at the intersection, signed as Byway to Snap & Ridgeway. Follow this track for 1.75 miles (2.8 km) to a junction beside a large field, where a hardcore byway goes right, climbing towards houses on the ridge (SU 227764).

This track is known locally as the Snape Road. Somewhere along here a minor skirmish occurred in September 1643, during the Civil War. A Parliamentary army of 10,000 was returning to London after the siege of Gloucester. Such a large column of troops was difficult to conceal, as it would have stretched for 3 or 4 miles. Not surprisingly, it was spotted by the Royalists, and a certain amount of fighting took place around Lower Lodge Barn. Some of the casualties were buried near Aldbourne, and were later interred in the churchyard, after being discovered during building excavations. Beyond the barn is High Clear Down nature reserve, home to a number of rare species in an area otherwise dominated by intensive farming. Now owned by the Wiltshire Wildlife Trust, it is an

Snow-covered landscape at Upper Upham

important site for the Early Gentian, a tiny spring flower that favours short turf on steep chalky hillsides.

3 To follow the short route, turn right to climb up to the houses at Upper Upham, emerging by the postbox in point 6. Otherwise, continue ahead for another 250m to a sharp left-hand bend facing a derelict wind pump. Just around the next bend is the site of the lost village of Snap, identified by a faded memorial stone beside the track.

SNAP. Throughout England some 7,000 sites exist where old villages have been abandoned. In Wiltshire there are known to be over a hundred. Many have virtually disappeared altogether, visible only from the air as irregular patterns in a field. Others can be identified on the ground as ridges and furrows, perhaps with piles of rubble where houses once stood. All too often the desertion was attributed to pestilence, such as the Black Death of 1348, or the Great Plague of 1665. But the true cause may lie elsewhere. Medieval villages were heavily dependent upon farming for their livelihood. Consequently, when vast areas of countryside were acquired by the Tudor sheep barons and turned into more lucrative pasture land, local employment vanished. Villagers were forced to leave in search of alternative work elsewhere, and many communities disappeared as a result.

Snap was somewhat different, for it survived the difficult farming conditions of the Middle Ages, only to succumb to the decline in arable farming in the late 19th century, when cheap imports of corn were pouring into the country. Its population of around 50 gradually drifted away, and when Snap Farm was vacated in 1905 only a handful of elderly residents remained. When the empty farm was subsequently bought by a local butcher, and turned into a sheep run, the new owner was unfairly blamed for the demise of the community. Even the local MP made the mistake of publicly speaking his mind, and later paid for his rash and inaccurate comments when he faced prosecution for slander. By the start of the First World War Snap was derelict, and being used for army training, causing more damage to the already ruined buildings. When author H W Timperley visited the site in 1935, he reported: '. . . the walls of Snap, the village in the hollow, are so crumbled and reduced that, together with the orchards and gardens round them, it cannot be long before a name is all that is left . . . who will walk along this narrow, bough-hidden lane without fear, not of the quiet ghost of Snap, but of the decay of downland life which unpeopled the village and left it waste?'

Today the site is overgrown, and marked only by a memorial stone placed beside the track in 1991 by children from Toothill school in Swindon. In winter clumps of snowdrops grow among the trees, and piles of moss-covered stones replace the cottages that once stood in this lonely place.

4 Continue along the same track past Snap, then at a byway junction go through the gate into an open field. Follow the track past the horse jumps, climbing gradually to another gate and junction. Continue ahead towards the mast, but before it turn right onto the Ridgeway (SU 213765).

5 Follow the Ridgeway northwards for 800m to a staggered crossroads (SU 213773). Turn right, then leave the Ridgeway by going straight on along a byway to Upper Upham.

The views from here are extensive, so it is easy to understand why Upper Upham disputes Baydon's claim to be the highest

Upham Court

village in Wiltshire. At 253m above sea level, it stands 20m higher than its rival, but is it large enough to be called a village? To the left of Upham Farm is the site of another deserted village, but there is no public access. Like Snap it was a farming community that lost its employment, and the population moved out. Upper Upham was once part of Aldbourne Manor, which in 1365 came into the possession of John of Gaunt, who effectively ruled England during the minority years of his nephew Richard II. Although he owned many estates throughout the country, he is known to have visited Upham several times for hunting. Local tradition claims that as there was no water supply in Upham, he had to go into Aldbourne to have a bath! The present manor house dates from around 1600, and for a while remained empty and derelict. It was discovered in 1907 by Edward Thomas, while researching his biography of Richard Jefferies, and he was so impressed by the views that he considered renting it. In the event the property was sold a few years later and subsequently restored.

6 Proceed along the concrete directly through Upham Farm, and onto a narrow tarmac road past houses and the green. The shortcut merges from the right by the postbox and byway sign. Continue along the fence-lined road to pass Upham Court on your left. After High Clear House turn right at the signpost by the gate (SU 232770). Follow the wide grass strip to a second gate, and keep straight on to a third. Now follow the rutted track all the way to the B4192 at New Barn, and retrace your route back into Aldbourne.

ALDBOURNE. Like many early settlements, Aldbourne suffered a number of disastrous fires throughout its history, due to the widespread use of timber and thatch. In 1760, fire destroyed 72 houses, together with barns full of corn and weaving materials. Worse followed a few years later when a hay rick caught fire during a hot dry summer. Fanned by a strong south-westerly wind, the flames spread through much of the village, engulfing 80 houses, 26 barns, and assorted farm machinery. An appeal was launched to raise funds for those who had lost all their possessions, and in 1778 two fire engines were obtained in case further fires broke out. Inevitably they did, such as in 1793 and 1817. Subsequent rebuilding in stone helped to reduce the risk, and after putting in a final appearance at a barn fire in 1921, the two fire engines were replaced by a more up to date machine that cost £40. Nicknamed Adam and Eve, the retired appliances are preserved in St Michael's church.

Further reading:

Muir, Richard, 1986, *The lost villages of Britain*. (Michael Joseph)

Watts, Kenneth, 1989, *Snap*. (Wiltshire C C)

Gandy, Ida, 1975, *The Heart of a Village*. (Moonraker Press)

Snowdrops in St Michael's churchyard, Aldbourne

9 Two Wiltshire Authors
South Marston and Sevenhampton
(5 miles/8 km)

(OS Explorer 170)

This level walk links together two Wiltshire villages that have opposing literary connections. South Marston will forever be associated with Alfred Williams, who spent almost his entire life here, mostly in hardship and poverty. Despite his obvious talent he never achieved the success he rightfully deserved, and outside Wiltshire remains largely unrecognized as a serious author. On the other hand, Sevenhampton was for a short time home to Ian Fleming, creator of the secret agent, James Bond. His lifestyle could not have been more different, but death, as they say, is a great leveller. Perhaps the only thing these two writers have in common is their final resting place - on Wiltshire soil, just a couple of miles apart.

Our walk passes both, as it follows minor tarmac roads and fieldpaths, and in the process goes through Roves Farm, where conservation and education are as much a part of the agenda as agriculture. Extend your walk by trying one of seven nature trails. Each is waymarked in a unique colour, and takes you in an anti-clockwise direction that ends back at the visitor centre. Here you can take refreshments before continuing your walk back to South Marston through a newly planted community

Alfred and Mary Williams on their honeymoon in 1903

51

woodland. Most of the walk is on public footpaths shown on the map, although at two locations it deviates along permissive paths for convenience.

---

1 **Start at South Marston village car park, adjacent to the primary school (SU 195879). Turn left past the school, then cross the road to visit St Mary Magdalen church.**

Entering the churchyard through the lych-gate, turn left to find the grave of Alfred and Mary Williams beneath a tall fir tree, a few metres from the church tower. Just along the road is Cambria Cottage, where Alfred was born, Rose Cottage, where he spent his childhood, Dryden House, where he and Mary began married life, and Ranikhet, the house he built himself. All, quite literally, within a stone's throw of each other.

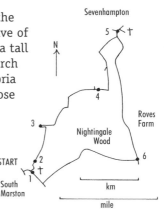

ALFRED WILLIAMS (1877-1930). Owen Alfred was the fifth child of Elias and Elizabeth Williams. At the age of 11 he left school to work for a local farmer. The wages were poor, so he joined his brothers at the railway works in Swindon. The pay may have been better, but the conditions were dreadful. In his spare time he sought every opportunity to educate himself, studying late into the night, absorbing everything he read, and eventually becoming fluent in five languages. They were not the qualifications for his job as a steam hammerman, but his heart was set on becoming a writer and poet. Despite failing eyesight, he started producing articles and poems for magazines, but there was little demand for this type of work. Undaunted, he persevered, and was often praised for his literary talent, even though it did not help to pay the household bills. His first book of prose - *A Wiltshire Village* - was an account of life in South Marston. But its honesty upset the vicar, whose sermons were criticised for being too long. Nevertheless, the book sold reasonably well, and encouraged Alfred to produce a similar book about other nearby villages. His best known book, *Life in a Railway Factory*, could not be published until after he had quit his job in the hot,

St Mary Magdalen church, South Marston

smoke-filled atmosphere that was gradually destroying his health. This too was an honest account of his own experiences, and hence was an outspoken condemnation of the conditions endured by thousands of his fellow workers. Readers were shocked, while critics applauded the author's courage. The railway authorities were not impressed. After wartime service in India, he returned home to build his own house using recycled bricks. More books followed, but his health continued to deteriorate, and when his wife fell ill, Alfred was distraught. They died within seven weeks of each other. Only now are we beginning to appreciate the quality of his writings, his vivid descriptions of everyday people, and his passionate understanding of the rigours of life. In *Poems in Wiltshire* he enthuses about the countryside he knew well, some of which we sample on this walk:

> Down by Sevenhampton's waving fields there flows
> A gentle-minded stream with steady motion,
> That underneath the emerald-tinted boughs
> Strives toward the drifting ocean.
>
> Dear winding river, companion of my thought,
> Whose flowery banks have shared my exultation,
> And now my years are with some sadness fraught,
> Dost pity my vexation.
>
> Long mayst thou wander under sun and shade
> And dream thy hours away in ease and leisure!
> May all thy summer flowers be re-arrayed
> In full, unstinted measure!

2 Facing the lych-gate in front of the church, look left for
a yellow arrow on the fence to the left of The Maples.
From here to Sevenhampton our route follows the
waymarkers for Heritage Trail 4. Cross the stream and turn
left to a gate as directed. Then turn right to a second gate
leading onto a fence-lined path across a paddock. At the
end cross a stile, and turn right along the edge of the field.
At the top, follow it around left to locate a gap in the
hedgerow (SU 196887).

Before going through the gap, turn round for a panoramic view
of the Ridgeway escarpment that extends from the Uffington
White Horse Hill in neighbouring Oxfordshire, across
Bishopstone to Foxhill, then Liddington Hill and Barbury
Castle, all favourite locations for Alfred Williams, that he
referred to in his books.

3 On the other side of the hedgerow, turn right to follow
the field edge on a permissive path. At the far end, bear
left to locate a stile in front of a pond in the adjacent field.
Go past the pond and continue alongside the field. Before
reaching some trees look for a gap in the hedge on your
right. Turn left beside the next field, where teasels grow,
and distant wind turbines can be seen. At the field corner,
continue ahead through an open gateway surfaced with
rubble. Fork right diagonally through a gap in the willow
plantation, as indicated by several waymarkers. Proceed
along the field edge beside a ditch, as far as a yellow
waymarker pointing left through a gap beneath an
overhanging tree (SU 205893).

4 The footpath continues along the left-hand edge of the
next field to a yellow waymarker on a post, where it
turns and crosses the field diagonally towards the church.
However, a better alternative is to turn right and follow the
perimeter around two sides of the field on a permissive path.
The two routes merge by a waymarker post in the hedgerow,
and continue to a kissing gate at the top corner of the field.
Proceed along the edge of the next field to a second kissing
gate, and immediately turn right, aiming for the church.
After a third gate, continue across two small fields to exit
onto Roves Lane. Turn left to visit the church, which is
accessed on foot by entering a private drive from the
triangular road junction (SU 208904), then going through a
small gate on your left in front of Sevenhampton House.

Sevenhampton church

IAN FLEMING (1908-1964). Son of an MP, and grandson of a Scottish banker, Ian Fleming was born into a lifestyle of wealth and privilege. At 13 he went to Eton, where he excelled at athletics, but not as a scholar. After a further unsuccessful period at Sandhurst, he completed his studies in Austria and Switzerland. Despite this he failed the entrance exam to join the foreign service, but later as a journalist with Reuters was posted to Moscow, where he became interested in politics. The experience led to a subsequent appointment as part of a trade delegation to Russia in 1939, which turned out to be an undercover mission. It made him an ideal candidate to take charge of secret wartime operations with British naval intelligence. One of them was code-named Goldeneye, a name that would subsequently be given to his house in Jamaica, as well as one of the James Bond novels that would eventually sell more than 100 million copies in 32 different languages. The hero, 007, was largely based on the author's own lifestyle, even though he was actually named after an American ornithologist.

A long private drive leads to Sevenhampton Place, a 40-bedroom mansion that was in a poor state of repair when first seen by Ann Fleming. Formerly called Warneford Place, the building was riddled with dry-rot, the gardens were overgrown, and the lake needed dredging. It was just the sort of project she needed to occupy her time while her husband was abroad researching more books. After four years of extensive rebuilding, the Flemings moved into their new home in 1963. By this time Ian Fleming was in poor health, and was destined to live here just a few months. Ann never recovered from the turmoil of his death, and the subsequent suicide of their son, Caspar. While the James Bond phenomenon continues to enthrall cinema audiences worldwide, the creator and his family remain in Wiltshire, their grave beside Sevenhampton church marked by a four-foot high obelisk. Look left as you enter the churchyard.

5 Leave the churchyard by retracing your steps to the road junction and into Roves Lane. Now follow the lane all the way to Roves Farm (SU 210888), and pick up a leaflet if you wish to take a detour around one of the farm trails. Access to them is just after the mast, where coloured arrows show the anti-clockwise routes, all of which return to the visitor centre car park. Then continue along the main track, and shortly after the mast turn right through the gateway, now again marked Heritage Trail 4.

ROVES FARM. Although still a working farm, much of the land has been set aside for wildlife, where children of all ages can learn about nature. You can lose yourself in the country's largest willow maze, take a tractor ride, or just stroll around one of the marked trails. For further inform-ation visit www.rovesfarm.co.uk or telephone 01793 763939 for opening times and current admission prices.

6 After passing a cottage, turn right at the crossing, and immediately left onto Nightingale Walk. At the hard track turn left past the farm (SU 203883), and continue down the lane to the main road. Turn right to return to South Marston village car park.

> NIGHTINGALE WOOD. Managed by the Forestry Commission, this 128-acre woodland was planted over a 5 year period from 1996, and forms part of the Great Western Community Forest. It is home to a wide variety of bird life that includes herons, woodpeckers and skylarks, as well as roe deer. Hard surfaced paths, with no gates or stiles, make it easily accessible to everyone. A car park is available if you wish to start this walk there (SU 206883). Access along Nightingale Lane, which is opposite the Village Hotel & Leisure Club on Old Vicarage Lane.

As you walk back to South Marston, the extensive Honda Motor works can be seen beyond the village. It stands on the site of a former wartime aircraft factory, built in 1940. To reduce the target for enemy air raids, some of the work was carried out at neighbouring sites in Blunsdon and Sevenhampton. The buildings were disguised with netting, and the concrete runways of the adjacent airfield were painted in camouflage colours. Even the grass was painted to simulate hedging when seen from above. After the war the factory was sold to Vickers, and continued in use for repairs and maintenance, as well as construction of new jet aircraft for the Royal Navy. The original factory was demolished in the 1980s, and has since been replaced by Honda's main European production line. Ironically, Swindon's railway works ceased production at about the same time. Had he been alive today, Alfred Williams may well have been employed at the factory right on his doorstep.

Further reading:

Clark, Leonard, 1969, *Alfred Williams, his life and work*. (David & Charles)

Davis, Michael Justin, 1981, *In a Wiltshire Village*. (Alan Sutton)

Lycett, Andrew, 1995, *Ian Fleming*. (Weidenfeld and Nicholson)

10 Wildlife by the Motorway

Lydiard Park and the M4

(6 miles/9.6 km)

(OS Explorer 169)

Walking beside a busy motorway is not everyone's idea of a peaceful stroll in the countryside. Depending on the wind direction, the constant traffic noise can easily be heard a couple of miles away. To avoid the M4 altogether would involve boycotting a long swathe of the landscape of North Wiltshire. That would be a great shame, for as we have seen in previous chapters, some of the finest scenery is within earshot of the motorway. Furthermore, wildlife often thrives where you would least expect it, and the undisturbed grassy banks and verges alongside main roads are an ideal habitat for both wildflowers and animals. Speeding by on the tarmac, you will rarely have the time or opportunity to see them. On foot, the possibilities are endless, and you may even find the wildlife coming to meet you.

Centred on the Lydiard villages to the west of Swindon, this level walk is predominantly on fieldpaths and hard tracks. Although best seen in summer, when the wildflowers are in full bloom, this time of year also produces long grass and a few overgrown sections, where dense brambles and tall nettles have to be negotiated. Hay fever sufferers beware. At the beginning and end of the walk, there is the opportunity to visit the house at Lydiard Park. The grounds are open daily until dusk, together with a cafe, which operates limited hours in winter. There are several other footpaths around the park, not included in this walk.

1 Lydiard Park is located off a minor road in West Swindon. From Blagrove roundabout on the A3102, turn onto the B4534 past Windmill Hill Business Park, then follow the brown signs for Lydiard <u>Park</u> (not House). There is ample free parking near the café (SU 101845). With your back to the café, follow the woodland path in front of you, to the right of the large notice board. This is the ornamental woodland walk, leading to the lakeside walk. Pass the picnic area and over the causeway between the two lakes. Turn left along the woodland path, then left again over the new dam at the top of the lake, aiming towards the house.

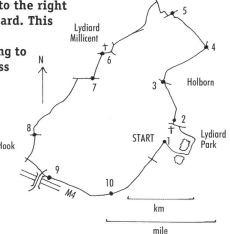

The splendid Palladian mansion in front of you could so easily have become just a pile of rubble. For more than five centuries it was owned by the St John family, who later took the name Bolingbroke. Various misfortunes and poor financial management left the family heavily in debt. The house gradually deteriorated, and when requisitioned by the military in 1942, its condition was so bad that troops billeted there

Lydiard House

preferred to occupy nearby huts rather than risk the house collapsing on them. Somehow the town clerk persuaded Swindon Corporation to take over the house and 147 acres of surrounding parkland. The purchase price of £4,500 may seem a bargain at today's prices, but in 1943 it was a massive amount to spend on a derelict place that appeared to have no future. Fortunately, it proved to be a wise decision. After much renovation, the house opened to the public in 1955, and since then work has continued, thanks to a £3million lottery grant. The lost lake has been reinstated by building a new dam; woodland walks and children's play area have been established, and new trees planted. At the back of the house, and almost part of it, is St Mary's church, praised by both Aubrey and Pevsner for its rich furnishings. You may wish to allocate some time at the end of your walk to examine it more closely.

2 **After crossing the dam, turn right at the church, then bear left around it to the entrance gate. In front of you is another car park, overlooking a large field. Follow the access road through the parking area to locate a gate in the fence, where there is a Millennium Trail yellow arrow. Enter the field and follow the hedgerow down the left-hand edge. Just before the bottom, look for a double stile on your left. Cross the next two fields diagonally, aiming for distant houses to locate a stile to the left of a gap in the hedge. Continue towards the houses, and exit by a stile in the corner onto the road at Holborn (SU 102855).**

Horses grazing at Lydiard Park

There may be horses grazing here among the buttercups, and dog roses hanging down from the hedgerows. Rabbits are often seen, and I have also spotted foxes rummaging around in the grass, not far from the houses. At this point our walk is following the Millennium Trail, a 28.5 mile (46.5 km) circular route that links central Swindon with surrounding farmland, as well as part of the Marlborough Downs. Look for the distinctive yellow waymarkers until just beyond the garden centre, then again towards the end of the walk, where we rejoin the trail.

3 Briefly continue along the road, then cross over to the footpath sign pointing along a concrete drive beside a house. At the end go through the gate in front of you, then left of the sheds onto a fence-lined path between a stream and paddock. Cross a stile into the field, and veer slightly right, under overhead cables. Then aim to the right of the line of fir trees that shelter a bungalow. In the fence look for a stile, followed by three more in quick succession. These take you across a narrow strip of grass, driveway, and paddock, and finally into a large open field. Aim diagonally left across the field to exit beside a house onto the road at Washpool (SU 109860).

4 Turn left along the road, then after crossing the bridge fork left at the bridleway sign onto a wide track that later narrows between hedges. Cross the next field towards an isolated gate at a gap in the hedgerow. Continue to another gate, and onto a track that leads to Stone Lane (SU 104866).

5 Turn left along the grass verge for about 100m, then cross over to the sign and stile on the opposite side. Go around the perimeter of the garden centre; continue beside a fence, then down the edge of a field beneath power cables. At the bottom ignore the stile where a Millennium Trail roundel points into the wood (SU 101867). Instead, keep to the bottom edge of the field, back under the power lines. At the far end ignore the opening on your right, and veer slightly left to locate an overgrown stile. Continue along the bottom edge of the next field, and follow it around left. Shortly before the houses, look for another stile on your right. Now parallel to the road, follow the top edge of two more fields, where wildflowers flourish in summer. Exit beside a red brick house (SU 097862) and continue straight on along the pavement.

This is Lydiard Millicent, named after Lady Milsent de Clinton, a former lady of the manor. Once a tiny settlement, it has grown in recent years, although still manages to remain separate from its much larger neighbour. Just around the corner is All Saints church. As we pass the churchyard, look for a cross which dates from the Saxon period.

6 Cross the road just before the junction, and turn left along Church Place. At the roundabout turn right, then just after passing the church turn left alongside the parish hall, signposted as Greatfield. Enter the field, and continue along the edge to a gate and stile with yellow arrows (SU 092856).

7 Cross the stile and turn right along the field edge. Take the left-hand fork at the next stile to cross the field diagonally. In the far corner is a stile where another footpath merges (SU 087853). Bear slightly left to a footbridge in the hedge, then aim to the right of the farm to locate a metal gate/stile. Fork left through a second gate, and along the farm track. Where it turns towards the farmyard, go straight on to the stile in the hedge. Continue across the next field to a gate, and exit onto the road (SU 083847). This is Hook Street.

8 Cross the road to the signpost opposite, and over the field. Look for a double stile in the hedgerow, which may be overgrown. Veer right to the next field corner, and over another stile. Continue along the left-hand edge of the next field until you reach a stile in the hedge on your left. Turn here to cross the adjacent field, aiming directly for the pylon (SU 084841).

Despite the proximity of the motorway, do not be surprised to see buzzards circling overhead. No longer a rare sight in England, these magnificent birds are certainly not confined to the quiet areas of the countryside. Nowadays they are regularly seen on fence posts beside a busy main road, or on the bare twisted branches of a dead tree, overlooking the grass verge. Providing the traffic keeps moving they are unconcerned; but approach on foot and they will take to the air long before you have a chance to see them close up.

Walking beside the motorway here one June day, I stopped to watch a buzzard being mobbed by a pair of crows. A few moments of fast and furious action followed, with each bird twisting and turning in mid-air. The conflict was short-lived, for as so often happens, the buzzard, despite its superior size, had enough commonsense to back off rather than risk injury. I was so pre-occupied with the activity overhead, that I was totally unprepared for what happened next. Suddenly there was a frantic scurrying in the undergrowth, and a brown hare burst out of the long grass right in front of me. For a second or two the startled animal froze, and just glared at me for intruding into its territory. Then, instead of running away, it headed straight towards me, veering away only at the last moment. With all this wildlife activity going on, I had overlooked the noise of the M4, proving, I suppose, that you can enjoy a walk beside a motorway if there are enough distractions to occupy your mind. Incredibly, there were more to follow as I continued with this walk.

9 Beside the M4 bridge, go under the cables and bear left to follow the edge of successive fields, alongside the motorway. After 700m bear left to go back under the power lines, aiming for a derelict barn (SU 093838).

The barn has seen better days! Cattle no longer shelter here, but it was an ideal hiding place for the barn owl that suddenly burst out from under the collapsed roof, just as I was passing. Then as I stood and watched it fly silently away, a young deer scurried through the bushes nearby. My arrival had clearly disturbed them both, yet the constant activity on the motorway had not bothered them at all.

10 Go past the barn, then bear left to locate a stile in the hedge. Follow the direction of the yellow arrow to a double stile on the far side of the next field. Keep to the right-hand side of two more fields to exit onto the road opposite the entrance to Lydiard Park.

Further reading:

Thamesdown, Borough of, 1996, *Lydiard House & Church*. (Dennis Print)
For opening times of Lydiard House, and other details, visit www.lydiardpark.org.uk

St Mary's Church, Lydiard Tregoze

11 Water, Water, Everywhere

Ashton Keynes and the Cotswold Water Park

(7.25 miles/11.6 km) or (8 miles/12.8 km)

(OS Explorer 169)

Straddling the Wiltshire/Gloucestershire border is Britain's largest water park, twice the size of the Norfolk Broads, and still growing. More than 50 years of sand and gravel extraction have created some 140 lakes across an area of 40 square miles (103 sq km), and estimates claim the industry here will continue for another half century. The result is a mecca for outdoor enthusiasts. Water sports include sailing, water-skiing and canoeing, while those seeking a more relaxing day can enjoy golf or angling. Off the water, walking and bird-watching are probably the most popular activities. This walk meanders around the lakes on the east side of Ashton Keynes, where refreshments are available at the White Hart or Horse & Jockey. The route is level throughout, but is often muddy, and the close proximity of the Thames can make some of

Observe the warning signs as you walk around the water park

it impassable after prolonged heavy rain. Much of the water park is still a working environment, and visitors need to be vigilant to vehicle movements around active quarries, as well as observing warning notices about quicksand. The main road through the park is the B4696, Spine Road, which connects to the A419 trunk road near the Gateway visitor centre, where cafe and other facilities are provided. Spine Road has a dedicated cycle path and pavement along much of its length.

1 Although the car park at Waterhay Bridge (SU 060933) is a convenient place to access this walk, it is susceptible to occasional flooding from the adjacent river. A drier, all weather alternative is the car park and picnic site at Clayhill Copse (SU 051952), alongside Spine Road East, two miles (3.2 km) from the A419/B4696 interchange. Here a footpath sign points to Ashton Keynes. Follow it to a gap in the trees, over the stile, and along the right-hand edge of the field. Keep right of the quarry workings to go around the lake as far as a kissing gate beside some fir trees. Go through the gate onto an enclosed path and around a house. Continue across the front of more houses, between upright stone slabs. The footpath emerges beside a garage onto Back Street.

As you enter Ashton Keynes you feel you are intruding into private gardens as you follow the footpath across the front of the houses. Small signs point you in the right direction, between upright limestone slabs, the county's highest concentration of 'gravestone' walling. Ashton Keynes is often referred to as the village of the crosses, for at some point around the 14th century four preaching crosses were erected, possibly to replace earlier examples dating from the Saxon period. During the Civil War all were badly damaged by passing troops, and over the years broken pieces were scattered around the village to be re-used in various ways. Then in 1917 one cross was restored, having been reassembled from all but one of its missing parts. It now stands in the churchyard as a war memorial. The path to it is lined with magnificent horse chestnut trees that provide a bumper crop of conkers each autumn. During the First World War local schoolchildren collected the conkers for the war effort. Together with acorns and fir cones, they were distilled to make acetone, a key ingredient of cordite.

In 1086, the Domesday Book referred to the village as Essitone. Since then the name has changed ten times. While Ashton means a settlement by an ash tree, Keynes was derived from William de Keynes, the lord of the manor in 1256, who changed his family name from Cahaignes, where it originated in Normandy. The manorial system prevailed here until 1913, when the estate was auctioned off to various buyers. At this time Ashton Keynes was still surrounded by lush water meadows, where cattle grazed and wildflowers grew in vast numbers, prompting Edward Hutton in his *Highways and Byways in Wiltshire* to refer to it as '. . . the very beautiful village . . . a little paradise with flowing waters everywhere . . .' Not long afterwards gravel extraction took over and the meadows started to disappear. Despite this the village itself continues to attract best kept village awards. Its greatest attraction is the infant river that flows down the centre of Church Walk, then alongside the main street, where access to properties is provided by individual bridges, famously referred to by Fred Thacker in 1908 as '. . . the perennial delight of Ashton Keynes.'

2 **To visit Ashton Keynes, turn right along Back Street. At the end turn left, then right into Church Walk to inspect this delightful corner of the village. Then return to the junction and follow the infant river along High Road. At the White Hart, turn left into Park Place, follow the road around, then next left into Fore Street, past the village shop. Finally turn left into Kent End to rejoin the main route at the bridge, where a Thames Path sign points along the stream.**

3 **To bypass the village centre, turn left along Kent End as far as the bridge over the tiny stream. A Thames Path sign points left, and from here we shall be following the national trail waymarkers until we reach the old railway line at point 5. In front of the farm entrance, go through the kissing gate to follow the field edge, then along a gravel drive between more houses to exit onto Rixon Gate. Cross the road, then over the sports field, in front of the pavilion, aiming for a gate. Continue ahead through Millennium Green, and emerge onto a fence-lined track that goes between two lakes (SU 056938). Follow it to a junction just before the car park at Waterhay Bridge (SU 060933).**

The river Thames flows under Waterhay Bridge, right beside the car park. Normally this is a quiet stretch of the river, and at times of drought is almost dry at this point, which is about 7

Some of the local wildlife

miles (11.2 km) from the river's source. However, during prolonged wet weather the shallow channel overflows onto the surrounding fields, so that much of the landscape here is under water, including all the footpaths.

RIVER THAMES.

This little stream, whose hamlets scarce have names,
This far-off, lonely mother of the Thames. (William Morris).

During the last ice age, the Thames may well have been a mile (1.6 km) wide as it laid down the gravel beds that are now quarried so extensively. Yet at that time it was not even a river in its own right, but merely a tributary of the Rhine, whose vast estuary extended all the way to Scotland. When the ice retreated Britain became an island, and the Thames we know today was born. The origins of its name, however, are still unclear. Some claim it was derived from the word Teme, meaning dark, although this also applies to other rivers with similar names. The first record of its name appeared in 55 BC, when Julius Caesar referred to it as Tamesis. Later, King Alfred called it Tames, and later still Elizabeth I used the spelling Themmes. Although much of the river's water originates in Wiltshire, the official source is to be found in neighbouring Gloucestershire, just north of Kemble. More often than not, however, the tiny spring at Thames Head is dry, activated only rarely during the wettest periods. In drought conditions the shallow channel may well be completely dry all the way to the Wiltshire border.

4 Turn left away from Waterhay Bridge car park. Then after 100m turn right to continue along the Thames Path as it meanders back and forth between various lakes.

The Thames Path national trail follows the river for 184 miles (294 km) from its official source to the Thames barrier at Woolwich. Its route is well signposted by the acorn symbol, and as far as possible remains on or near the riverbank. The next mile or so (1.6 km), is an exception, as the trail briefly moves away from the river to take us around several consecutive lakes. Path and river are reunited near a small two-arch bridge, and in flood conditions this whole area will be under water, or at least very muddy. Along this section look out for wildlife and waterfowl. There are many resident species, plus winter visitors that include large flocks of lapwing and golden plover.

5 Leaving the lakes behind for a while, keep following the Thames Path signs, ignoring a track going off to the right. After 2.5 miles (4 km) from Waterhay Bridge, we arrive at a T-junction where a muddy bridleway goes left to South Cerney. Turn right here, towards Cricklade, then after about 150m climb up to the elevated trackbed of the old railway line (SU 080949). This is the same railway we first encountered in chapter 4. Leave the Thames Path here, by turning left along the trackbed, which is now part of National Cycle Route 45. Shortly after going under a red brick bridge, a footpath from Cerney Wick joins from the

Quarry workings near Ashton Keynes

right. Then after a further 280m look on your left for a footbridge with a stile at either end (SU 068958).

6 Cross the bridge and follow the left-hand edge of the field around to a gate and stile. Continue across the next field, keeping close to the hedge, and emerge onto Wickwater Lane (SU 066954). Briefly turn right, then go left over the stile where a sign points to Ashton Keynes. Keep to the left-hand edge of the next field. At the far end cross another stile onto a fence-lined path that goes back and forth around more lakes, over a stream, and finally exits near a quarry onto Friday's Ham Lane (SU 059951).

7 Our onward route is just across the road, on the other side of the hedgerow, but there is no access to it from here. Instead, turn left along the pavement for 500m to the minor road junction near more quarries (SU 060946). Cross the main road into the gateway opposite, beside a footpath sign to Ashton Keynes. Then immediately turn right through a gap in the hedge, and follow the signs along the perimeter of the quarry, now going back in the opposite direction, parallel to the road. This is still an active quarry, so be prepared for slight variations of the route as digging progresses. Stay beside the hedge until you reach a stream, directly opposite the point where you first emerged onto the road. Turn here, keeping the stream on your left, to follow the field edge. Cross a quarry road, and continue to a gap in the trees that leads back into the car park.

Further reading:

Petersen, Madge & Ward, Ernie, 1986, *Ashton Keynes: A Village with No History.* (Keith Cowley)
Sharp, David, 2005, *The Thames Path.* (Aurum Press)
For further details of the Cotswold Water Park visit www.waterpark.org

12 Wildflowers and Waterways

Cricklade and the Upper Thames

(5 miles/8km choice of 2 routes) or (9.5 miles/15.2km)

(OS Explorer 169)

When William Cobbett rode through the river Thames at Cricklade in 1826 he famously declared that it was 'not above four or five yards wide, and not deeper than the knees of my horse.' Clearly he chose to cross the river during one of its quieter moments, for long before climate change became part of everyday vocabulary, the upper Thames and its tributaries regularly flooded the fields all around here. From nature's point of view this was not always a bad thing, as we shall discover. On the other hand, waterlogged fields do not make comfortable walking, and at worst may prove to be impassable. Take care, therefore, to choose dry conditions for this walk, which can be divided into three separate options:-

Northern route – 5 miles/8 km.
Southern route – 5 miles/8 km.
Combined route – 9.5 miles/15.2 km.

The Northern route is fairly straightforward, but the Southern route will present a greater challenge for your navigational skills. All of the fields are prone to flooding, and may remain waterlogged for some time after the river levels have subsided. For convenience, each walk begins and ends in the centre of Cricklade, where there is free parking at different locations, and plenty of pubs in the main High Street.

1 If you have not visited Cricklade before, simply aim for the tall, distinctive tower of St Sampson's church. Nearby, a small car park is situated beside the Town Hall in the lower half of the High Street. Space here is limited; alternative parking is available at Fairview Fields, off Stockham Close, a short distance from the A419 interchange as you enter Cricklade on the B4040. This will involve an extra 500m walk to the town centre along Calcutt Street/B4040. Roadside parking can also be found at the top end of the High Street. All three walks start beside the Jubilee Clock, which stands in front of the Vale Hotel, at the junction of Calcutt

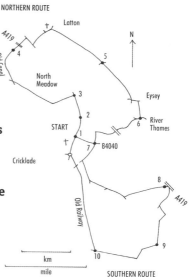

Street and High Street (SU 100936). To follow the Southern route, walk along Calcutt Street for 350m to Spital Lane, turn right, then continue the directions from Point 7.

2 To follow the Northern route or Combined route, start by walking up the High Street to the top end, where the road crosses the infant Thames at North Wall and heads out of town along an old Roman causeway. Continue along the pavement to Weavers Bridge (SU 100944), where a Nature Reserve notice stands beside a gate at the entrance to North Meadow.

> NORTH MEADOW. Situated between the infant Thames and the river Churn, this 108 acre meadow is internationally important for its extensive collection of wild flowers. One in particular attracts many visitors from far and wide. A century ago, the Snake's Head Fritillary (Fritillaria meleagris) grew all over southern England, but intensive farming since 1940 has eradicated many sites. A few small collections survive across the middle of the country, but Wiltshire is the exception, with one-third of all UK sites. The largest, by far, is North Meadow, which contains around 1.5 million plants – 80% of the entire British population, and probably the largest site of its kind in Europe. It owes its success to the regular winter flooding that not only produces rich alluvial silt, but over

the centuries has made it unsuitable for farming, leaving the wild flower roots undisturbed. For 2 or 3 weeks around the end of April, North Meadow is a haze of purple as the delicate fritillaries come into flower, with a few contrasting white blooms here and there. By late June the fritillaries have sown their seeds and given way to other species. Then, in accordance with ancient traditions applicable to Lammas Land, a hay crop is cut before 12th August, after which grazing is permitted until 12th February.

3 Enter the nature reserve, go past another notice board and through the kissing gate. Follow the faint path directly across the meadow, passing a marker post and over a concrete bridge spanning a shallow ditch. Before reaching the river, turn right at another marker post, to walk along the edge of the meadow parallel to the line of trees on your left. Ignore a footpath going off left over a low bridge. At the far end, where the river bends left under a footbridge, climb the steps, over the stile, and turn right through the gate (SU 088947). Leaving the river, bear right onto a narrow path through bushes, alongside the overgrown bed of an old canal.

This is the former North Wilts canal, which opened in 1819 to link the Wilts & Berks canal in Swindon with the Thames & Severn canal at Latton. All of these waterways lost their trade to the railways and had become derelict by the early 20th century. In recent years efforts to restore them have been underway at several locations, and part of the canal bed has been cleared at The Basin, where the North Wilts joined the Thames & Severn.

4 At Basin Cottage follow the path to the right, over the bridge, and out along the entrance drive. Proceed towards the traffic noise and cross the bridge over the dual carriageway. Continue down the narrow road to the T-junction and turn right along the pavement into Latton village. This is the route of the original A419, which overlaid the Roman road, Ermin Way. After 150m turn left into Gosditch, beside a medieval preaching cross. At the far end, go right of the church into a no through road, leading to a gate where a bridleway begins. On the other side of the gate, fork right through a second gateway onto a signed footpath. The right of way bears left of the concrete

River Thames east of Cricklade

and crosses the field to a stile over a ditch halfway along the far side, waymarked by a yellow arrow (SU 097957). From here, follow the hedgerow along the right-hand side of three successive fields for 950m, to finally exit through a kissing gate onto a minor road at Sheeppen Bridge (SU 105952).

5 As indicated, follow the zig-zag route over the road and down the other side to a kissing gate, to continue in the same general direction along the right-hand edge of another field. On your right is a sand and gravel quarry, and shortly we pass under a low bridge carrying a conveyor belt. Cross a stile into the next field, still beside the stream. Exit through a gate near a house, where a footpath sign points ahead into an overgrown area of scrub. Avoid this by turning left along the rough tarmac road for 150m to a gateway/stile on your right, just before the farm. A yellow arrow points straight across the field. Aim slightly to the right of the distant phone mast to locate a footbridge over the Thames (SU 113941). Just before it is a stile in a wire fence. Cross the river and turn right along the Thames Path.

Centuries ago, the river here was navigable for large vessels. Indeed, old chronicles claimed that the Vikings sailed their longships up the Thames as far as Cricklade. The river remained the preferred trade route until 1789, when the Thames & Severn canal opened, after which the Thames gradually became

73

overgrown. Despite this, in 1984 attempts were made to restore navigation to Cricklade by sailing a loaded barge upstream. Although it succeeded in reaching its destination, the highly publicised event failed to sway public opinion.

6 Follow the Thames Path waymarkers beside the river and under the A419 bridge. Cross the side stream to emerge on a large open green (Fairview Fields) near the alternative car park. Stay beside the river until you pass a footpath sign, then turn left along the field edge to the houses, and continue down the tarmac path alongside No 21. This leads to Calcutt Street. Turn right to return to the Jubilee Clock, and the end of the Northern route. To continue with the Combined route, cross Calcutt Street into Spital Lane, signed as a bridleway. The Southern route joins us here (SU 104935).

Fairview Fields, Cricklade

7 Walk to a gate at the end of Spital Lane, enter the field and follow the hedgerow. Proceed through two more gates, then immediately after the next, turn left over the stile (SU 101931). Follow the yellow arrow diagonally across the field to locate a double stile in the hedgerow, leading into the next field. Continue to a visible gap in the hedge, where a bridge crosses a stream. Up to this point our route has been parallel to the old railway embankment, a short distance away on our right-hand side. We now move away from it by taking the left-hand fork at a footpath junction, across the centre of the field. Aim for the corner of a low hedge at a dip in the ground, then alongside the hedge, directly towards the distant mast. Cross another stile where a wide grass bridleway joins from the right (SU 105927). Turn left to a gate, then along the next field edge, beside a hedgerow. Part of the way along here look for a gate on your right, where a bridleway arrow points left to a second gate. Cross the next field diagonally towards a large tree. Go through another gate and turn left. For the next 850m proceed in a straight line along the edge of successive fields, beside hedges and through more gates. Finally exit onto the A419 at the Kingshill Recycling Centre (SU 118927).

8 Turn right along the grass verge, then immediately after crossing the depot entrance, go through the gate with a blue arrow on the post. Follow the track between fences, with the river Ray on your left. Go through the left-hand of two more gates, to continue on a wide grass strip between hedges. At a junction with several gates (SU 117923), pass through the first gate and immediately turn left on another grass strip between tree plantations. At the end of this section is another gate. Turn right, then go around a left-hand bend onto a long straight section of 500m. Shortly before it ends is an open clearing, with a gap in the hedgerow on your right. Walk through the gap and immediately turn left, to continue along the other side of the hedgerow (SU 116915).

The route through the tree plantations can be a little confusing in places, as there are no traditional signs to guide you. However, a number of posts carrying waymarkers produced by the Country Landowners Association can be found at strategic locations.

9 After 100m fork right through the trees, beneath cables, and straight on along another wide grass strip. At the next junction turn left through a gap and along the edge of the plantation with an open field on your left. At the end, exit the tree plantation at a gate (SU 113912), and turn right along a wide rutted track that is likely to be muddy. This is South Meadow Lane. Follow it for 800m.

As you progress, look left to an assortment of wagons and carriages stabled at Hayes Knoll, the northern terminus of the Swindon and Cricklade Railway. Eventually this preserved line will be extended in both directions as part of the Cricklade

The lower end of Cricklade High Street, and the landmark tower of St Sampson's church

Country Way project – a green corridor that will one day provide a choice of recreational transport links from Swindon to the Cotswold Water Park – steam railway, canal, cycle route and footpaths. The northern extension of the railway currently ends at South Meadow Lane.

10 On reaching the railway trackbed (SU 105914), turn right through the gate and follow it all the way to Cricklade, signed as National Cycle Route 45. Emerging on the road in Cricklade, go over the roundabout and follow the High Street back to the town centre.

Further reading:

Stretton, John, 2003, *The Swindon and Cricklade Railway*. (Past & Present)

Dalby, L J, 2000, *The Wilts and Berks Canal*. (Oakwood Press)

13 Escape to the Country

Broad Hinton and Broad Town

(8.25 miles/13.2 km)

(OS Explorer 157)

Anyone interested in historical buildings will be familiar with the remarkable series of books by Sir Nikolaus Pevsner. Less widely known is the fact that the author often escaped the busy city for the peace and quiet of an isolated cottage at Broad Town, and was subsequently buried nearby. The cottage was owned by Geoffrey Grigson, another prolific writer, who is chiefly remembered for his travel guides, and countryside and wildlife books, although many will recall his critical assessment of poetry. This walk takes us past their cottage, which is almost hidden at the base of the long escarpment that extends from Compton Bassett to Bincknoll Castle, with extensive views across the north Wiltshire plain. Cut into the steep chalk cliff above the cottage is the Broad Town white horse, and we shall also have distant views of its stable companion on Hackpen Hill. Refreshments are available at the Crown Inn, near the end of the walk, and just off our route at the Goddard Arms in Clyffe Pypard.

1 The walk starts beside St Peter ad Vincula church in Broad Hinton (SU 106763). Access is from a triangular junction on Summers Lane/High Street, where a narrow lane goes behind St Peter's Cottages. A rough parking area can be found to the left of the lychgate. Nearby, a faded signpost points along the wide grass area towards a gap in the tall trees at the far end. Emerging through the gap, turn right along a wide grass track, between fence and trees. Follow it all the way around, behind private gardens,

and along a gravel/tarmac drive to exit onto the road at a bend. Turn left onto the signposted byway.

This is Vize Lane, or Way, part of an ancient trading route that once connected Wroughton to Devizes. In places the surface is deeply rutted, and hence muddy and waterlogged at times, although its width allows you to bypass the worst parts. However, in wet conditions you can expect to accumulate a thick layer of mud on the soles of your boots before you reach the road at Lambourne Ground. The map shows a stone circle here, but there is nothing to see, apart from a solitary sarsen slab on the bank overlooking the road junction.

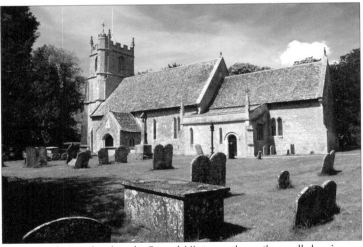

St Peter ad Vincula church, Broad Hinton, where the walk begins

2 Follow the byway for 1500m to emerge onto a minor road junction at Lambourne Ground (SU 092755). Continue ahead along the no through road for 1250m, where it ends beside two houses, and enters Whyr Farm.

3 In front of the first house (SU 083747) turn right into the field, and cross it towards the distant mast. At the top end bear right then left to cross the centre of the next

Sarsen stone on the Vize Way at Lambourne Ground

field, now slightly to the right of the mast. The path
continues in the same direction across another field,
climbing gently to provide wide views back to the Ridgeway
escarpment. Go through a gap in the hedgerow and proceed
ahead over the next field. At the end of this last field the
map appears to show the path going through the wood in
front of you, and over private property. However, a more
convenient permissive path has been created, allowing us
to go to the right of the trees and along the field edge,
thus bypassing the thatched farmhouse. We emerge in
front of the farm gate, and continue along the gravel track
to exit at the road junction (SU 077765), above Clyffe
Pypard.

4 Turn right along the road to the first bend, crossing
over to the left-hand side before you reach it, as
visibility is restricted. A bridleway sign points straight
ahead along the field edge. Continue over a path junction,
then bear left to drop down from the field onto a narrow
sunken track that may be muddy in places. Exit by a
thatched cottage (SU 087773) and proceed down the tarmac
lane. At the junction beside Springfield House, turn right
along Pye Lane.

The Broad Town white horse is now clearly visible directly in
front of you. Although one of the less well known and least
visited of the county's chalk figures, nevertheless it still retains
an element of mystery about its origins. According to the Rev

Plenderleath, Rector of Cherhill in the 19th century, it was cut in 1864 by William Simmonds, the owner of Littletown Farm at the time. However, an alternative version was published in 1919 by the Curator of the Imperial War Museum. He claimed that as a schoolboy he helped to scour the horse in 1863, when it was apparently already 50 years old. Like all chalk carvings, the horse needs regular maintenance, and in the past has not always received it. As a result it had almost become invisible by 1991 when a local restoration group was established. Since then the horse has received more attention, and is best viewed at a distance rather than close up.

5 Emerge onto the main village road at a crossroads. On your left is Broad Town Farmhouse. Cross over into Chapel Lane. Where it bends to the right, continue ahead on a rough track between two elevated bungalows, signed as a public footpath. Follow the track to the isolated Littletown Farmhouse, which is directly below the white horse. On their right is a partly hidden cottage (SU 097782).

GEOFFREY GRIGSON (1905-1985). The son of a Cornish vicar, Geoffrey Grigson came to prominence in the 1930s as a writer, poet and editor of a poetry magazine *New Verse*. He was a noted critic and reviewer, but was frequently outspoken to the point where he caused offence to many of his contemporaries. His wide knowledge and literary expertise extended to many other subjects, particularly the countryside and natural history, as well as travel guides. In 1936 he bought and renovated a semi-derelict cottage adjacent to Littletown Farmhouse. It was an ideal rural retreat from his London home, and a decade later when he moved to Broad Town Farmhouse, he let the cottage to his city neighbour, Nikolaus Pevsner.

SIR NIKOLAUS PEVSNER (1902-1983). Born in Leipzig, Nikolaus Pevsner occupied several academic posts in Germany until 1933, when he was suspended from lecturing due to his Jewish background. He emigrated to England to escape Nazi persecution, and became a British citizen in 1946. As an acknowledged expert on art and architecture, he soon obtained a number of university positions in London and Cambridge. Although he produced a number of books, his greatest legacy is the 46-volume series of county guides 'The Buildings of England'. This monumental project occupied all his spare time, and is widely recognised as one of the greatest achievements of art scholarship. He was a workaholic and a keen walker, often travelling long distances to visit a remote building. Although he lived in London from 1941 to his death, he became a regular visitor to Wiltshire after 1946 as the guest of Geoffrey Grigson, whose cottage at Littletown became Pevsner's country retreat. Nikolaus and Lola Pevsner are buried in the churchyard at nearby Clyffe Pypard, where the gates are carved with their initials.

6 Arriving at the farmhouse, go through the first gate, then the next gate on your left, bearing a yellow arrow. Now follow a faint grass path across the top of the hillside, at the foot of the escarpment. At a path junction beneath overhanging trees, go through the gate ahead of you. From here proceed more or less straight on across successive fields, all the time parallel to the trees and escarpment on your right. In places the path may be concealed by long grass; beware of hidden dips in the surface. After about 1400m a farmhouse appears down to the left. Aim for the gate in the hedgerow ahead of you (SU 107795), and go through it. Immediately turn right onto a wide track that climbs steeply up to the ramparts of an old hillfort.

The track to Littletown Farmhouse, the white horse, and the Grigson-Pevsner cottage

This is Bincknoll Castle (pronounced 'Bynol'), an Iron Age hillfort on a chalk promontory with steep slopes on three sides. During the Norman period it was adapted as a motte and bailey castle, but all trace has since disappeared, possibly caused by subsequent landslips to which this hilltop is particularly susceptible.

7 Our route now follows the waymarkers of the White Horse Trail all the way to Broad Hinton. On reaching the top of the climb, cross the centre of the hillfort to a gate, where an arrow points straight on along the field edge. Continue alongside trees on a wide hard track until it bends sharply right. Go through the gate/stile, and cross the centre of the field, aiming for the right-hand end of the group of trees on the left. Here you will find two gates separating a narrow strip of land (SU 109779). Go through both gates and continue in the same direction across two more large fields, to finally exit onto the road beside a house (SU 112770).

8 Briefly turn left towards the A4361 junction, but before it cross the stile on the right to enter the field. Bear right to walk the length of the field, then over a farm track at two stiles part way along the fence. Aim for a gate in the far corner of the next field, near houses. Cross the stile and walk the short distance along the field edge to locate another stile in the hedge. Turn left along the tarmac path between high fences. Emerge in front of entrance gates, and turn left along a rough driveway. Exit onto Post Office Lane and turn right to return to the triangular junction on Summers Lane.

Further reading:

Pevsner, Nikolaus, 1963 and later, *The Buildings of England – Wiltshire*. (Penguin Books)

Grigson, Geoffrey, 1950, *The crest on the silver: an autobiography*. (Cresset)

14 A Seaside Adventure

Coate Water and Hodson

(5.5 miles/8.8 km)

(OS Explorer 169)

*Wiltshire has been described by numerous writers over the years.
Some were born here, others were attracted by the countryside
and became long-term visitors. Their various legacies have given
us an understanding of life in past times, and none more so than
Richard Jefferies. This semi-rural walk begins near his birthplace,
and explores some of the area where he grew up, and which he
subsequently wrote about in his books.*

*Created in 1822 as a reservoir to
supply the Wilts & Berks canal, today
Coate Water is the centrepiece of a
popular country park on the edge
of the sprawling town of Swindon.
A few steps along the road from
its entrance is Coate
farmhouse, now a museum
dedicated to Richard Jefferies.
As well as displays of his books,
manuscripts, and family
memorabilia, parts of the house
have been restored to reflect the
period of his birth.*

Richard Jefferies

1 **Access to the large free car
park is from the A4259/
B4006 roundabout (SU 177830). Walk
through to the lake near the diving
platform, and turn left along the concrete embankment,
signed to Chiseldon. Continue around the lake shore and
past the children's play area, on a tarmac/hardcore track.**

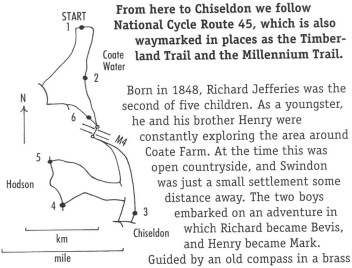

From here to Chiseldon we follow National Cycle Route 45, which is also waymarked in places as the Timberland Trail and the Millennium Trail.

Born in 1848, Richard Jefferies was the second of five children. As a youngster, he and his brother Henry were constantly exploring the area around Coate Farm. At the time this was open countryside, and Swindon was just a small settlement some distance away. The two boys embarked on an adventure in which Richard became Bevis, and Henry became Mark. Guided by an old compass in a brass case, and a map that was just a large sheet of brown paper, they sailed down the Mississippi on a raft built from an old packing case, made watertight by plugging the holes with moss, clay and old handkerchiefs!

'We will find a new sea where no one has ever been before,' proclaimed Bevis. 'Look! there it is.'

Wiltshire's 'new sea' was of course Coate Water, fed by a tiny stream that became the Mississippi in the boys' imagination. In later years this epic adventure became the basis for a Richard Jefferies novel, once claimed to be the best boys' book ever written. The names may have changed, but some of the locations can still be identified around Coate Water. The same applies to many of Jefferies' novels, each drawing on the experience he gained wandering around the hills and fields, absorbing everything he saw in the countryside.

2 Continue over the bridge where the lake divides, and bear left along the cycle path all the way to the M4. Cross the curly-whirly bridge (SU 179812), and stay on the tarmac cycle path through the woodland until you reach a rough track, where the tarmac ends. Fork left along the main track, ignoring footpaths to left and right. The surface deteriorates as you climb up to emerge beside an open field. Shortly afterwards we arrive at a distorted T-junction (SU 184800), where we leave the cycle route as it turns sharp left into Chiseldon.

This is another section of the old Midland & South Western Junction Railway (see Chapter 4), which was partly overlaid by the motorway in 1971. The line continued into Chiseldon, where the old station site is now an open space with parking, in front of the Elm Tree Inn. When the railway opened here in 1881 a public holiday was declared, and local schoolchildren gathered to welcome the arrival of the first train. By this time, Richard Jefferies had married Jessie Baden in the nearby church. Initially they lived in Swindon, and in the same year his first two novels were published.

Coate Water

Neither generated many sales, but demand for his routine work as a journalist gained momentum, and in 1877 he and Jessie moved to Surbiton to be nearer his London publishers. Although he was destined never to return to live in his native county, he took with him a wealth of local knowledge that later enabled him to write extensively about the countryside he had left behind.

3 Turn right along the rough stony track, and within 100m exit onto the road at a bend. Immediately turn right at the Coate Water signpost, along a concrete drive to a house. As instructed, bear left of the private gateway, through a small lychgate, and onto a tree-lined path in a narrow hollow, descending all the way to a kissing gate. Walk ahead to the line of bushes at the bottom (SU 183803). Without crossing the stream, turn left at the waymarker post to follow the fence/hedgerow along the valley floor, aiming for the distant houses on the ridge.

The secluded Hodson valley

This is the secluded Hodson valley, hidden from the outside world and accessible only on foot. A romantic hideaway, where you can briefly escape the pressures of modern life – the sort of place you would expect to read about in a Jefferies' novel:

> If we had never before looked upon the earth, but suddenly came to it man or woman grown, set down in the midst of a summer mead, would it not seem to us a radiant vision? The hues, the shapes, the song and life of birds, above all the sunlight, the breath of heaven, resting on it; the mind would be filled with its glory, unable to grasp it, hardly believing that such things could be mere matter and no more. Like a dream of some spirit-land it would appear, scarce fit to be touched lest it should fall to pieces, too beautiful to be long watched lest it should fade away.

4 **Cross a bridge/stiles, then as you approach the end of the valley, look to your right for another footpath joining through two gates over the stream. At this point fork left across the valley to locate a gap in the trees, where a Millennium Trail waymarker on a post directs you along a raised path, that climbs up to the Calley Arms and exits beside the pub car park. Turn right along the narrow road through the village for about 600m, taking care to keep to the correct side at blind bends for the best visibility. After crossing a narrow bridge over a stream, the road climbs up to a bend. Just before the bend is a footpath sign on the right, beside a gate. On the opposite side of the road is a thatched cottage (SU 173808).**

The keeper's cottage stands in a sheltered 'coombe', or narrow hollow of the woodlands, overshadowed by a mighty Spanish chestnut, bare now of leaves, but in summer a noble tree. The ash wood covers the slope at the rear; on one side is a garden, and on the other a long strip of meadow with elms.

Richard Jefferies became friendly with the gamekeeper at Hodson, and the thatched cottage he describes in *The Gamekeeper at Home* seems almost unchanged, still dwarfed by the chestnut tree in its secluded setting.

5 **Go through the gate and bear left uphill on a sunken track. At the top, ignore the stile on your left, and continue ahead along the edge of the wood, where in spring bluebells grow extensively. Go through a kissing gate, then proceed in the same direction along the field edge, with Liddington Hill ahead in the distance. Ignore a waymarked footpath going off right, steeply downhill. Stay alongside the field until you reach a kissing gate in the corner, where a yellow waymarker directs you along a narrow path, keeping the fence on your left. This leads to a junction in a small hollow (SU 182805). Turn left through the kissing gate, then uphill to a 3-way wooden signpost. Bear left towards Coate Water, along the top edge of an open field, with the hospital clearly visible, and behind it the distant wind turbines at Watchfield. Reaching the trees, bear left to a waymarker post, then through the wood to a kissing gate. Cross the field diagonally to another gate in the opposite corner. Re-join the tarmac cycle path, and cross the M4 again on the curly-whirly bridge (SU 179812).**

6 **On the other side of the motorway, turn left through the kissing gate. Cross the centre of the field, going under the power lines between the two central pylons, aiming for a double gate at a gap in the hedgerow. As directed, bear left towards the right-hand of three prominent trees, where a signpost points left through two kissing gates. Exit onto the road (SU 175816), and turn right along it. Immediately before the next bend, turn right through the trees to enter the country park on a walkway, and follow the track parallel to the road. Fork right over the stream and along a wide avenue of trees, then follow the lakeside path back to the car park.**

> They left the shore awhile, and went into the quarry . . . when
> they looked round over the ocean they were quite alone: there was
> no one in sight either way, as far as they could see; nothing but
> the wall of sand behind, and the wide, gleaming water in front.

Bevis and Mark continue their adventures throughout many
chapters as they circumnavigate the 'new sea' in much the same
way as we have during this walk, albeit without the numerous
hazards encountered by the intrepid youngsters. You can learn
more about Richard Jefferies by paying a visit to the museum
at Coate Farm, which he lovingly referred to as 'the old house'.
In *The Life of The Fields* he described how it 'stood by a silent
country road, secluded by many a long, long mile, and yet
again secluded within the great walls of the garden.' His 'silent
country road' is now a busy dual carriageway, but within 'the
great walls of the garden' some measure of peace is available to
visitors.

In an unfinished account of his old home, not published
until the centenary of his birth, he left a piece of prose that
many feel epitomises his love of nature, and his affinity with
his inner self. Yet there is one other book that has always stood
out as the key to his true thoughts on life, and his obsessive
search for something out of reach. To fully appreciate it, we
need to visit Liddington Hill in the next chapter.

Further reading:

Selected books by Richard Jefferies (1848-1887):
Bevis: The Story of a Boy
The Gamekeeper at Home
Wild Life in a Southern County
The Amateur Poacher
Amaryllis at the Fair
Hodge and His Masters
Round About a Great Estate

THE RICHARD JEFFERIES MUSEUM. Located beside the
A4259 near the Day House Lane junction, the museum is
open on selected days, currently 1st and 3rd Sundays of
each month between May and September (2-5pm), and
on the 2nd Wednesday of each month (10-4pm). For the
latest details, telephone Swindon Museum on 01793
466556, or contact the Richard Jefferies Society on
01793 783040. Admission is free. Park at Coate Water.

15 To Eternity and Beyond

Liddington Hill and Sugar Hill

(5.25 miles/ 8.4 km)

(OS Explorer 157 and part of 170)

Much has been said and written about nature and the English countryside. Libraries are full of books on the subject, but few can rival the unique style of Richard Jefferies. Although his novels were not always well received, his natural history books about Wiltshire in the 19th century are unsurpassed. Yet, despite his literary talent, even he had to admit that some of his most intimate experiences with nature could not be properly expressed in words. Constantly he found himself searching for something that was unattainable, which he referred to as 'the Beyond', and this became the theme of his spiritual autobiography. Once started, The Story of My Heart *becomes compulsive reading, yet is not an easy book to understand. In places very intense, and even disturbing, it largely describes his somewhat unreal experiences on Liddington Hill, the subject of this walk. From a navigational point of view, it is an easy route to follow, with plenty of signs and waymarkers in all the right places. Some of the tracks are uneven and deeply rutted, and there are steep climbs at two locations, but the effort is well worthwhile for the extensive views available at the top. Other experiences are not guaranteed!*

---

1 Park in one of the laybys on the B4192 in Shipley Bottom (SU 230786), three miles (4.8 km) north-west of Aldbourne. About 100m away the road is crossed by a byway, where a sign points towards Peaks Down. Go through the gate, and follow the wide rutted track up to the top of

the Sugar Hill escarpment (SU 237787). The final part of the climb is fairly steep.

'Nowhere in all Wiltshire are the downs more spacious, more airily patterned in their shapes and more fluid in line than from Sugar Hill,' wrote H J Massingham in *English Downland*, describing the view from it as '. . . the still but unquiet sea of giant trough and mighty fold and greater billow, the great green sea of Wiltshire . . . to walk whose waves, restless in endless variation, yet brings tranquillity of spirit.'

Such eloquent praise is not exaggerated; the widespread panorama is ample reward for the steep climb, and the views continue as we follow the easy path along the ridge. Incidentally, the name has no connection with sweetener, but seems to be derived from Segur, a local landowner in the 12th century.

The track up to Sugar Hill

2 **At the top go through the first gate, and immediately turn left through the second, signed as a bridleway. Now follow the wire fence along the ridge, passing through several more gates/gateways, and clearly waymarked.**

Horses often graze on the steep hillside above Liddington Warren Farm. Just beyond is the distinctive beech clump on

Liddington Hill, more familiar from the other side to thousands of motorists on the M4. Over to your right is the Fox Hill transmitter, on the other side of Wanborough Plain.

3 After a mile (1.6 km) the bridleway gradually descends, turning to meet up with the Aldbourne road, then running parallel to it along the field edge. Near the large road signs, look for a gap in the fence, and step up to the road (SU 218804). Carefully cross over and continue up the gravel track opposite, signed as Ridgeway to Liddington Castle.

The steep climb eases as you draw level with the beech clump, together with its old gun emplacement. Soldiers on wartime duty here would have had early sightings of approaching enemy aircraft, so it is hardly surprising that many centuries earlier our Neolithic ancestors had built a hillfort on this elevated plateau. The path to it is not a public right of way (hence is not shown on OS maps), but the landowner has granted access for pedestrians.

4 On reaching a gate where the Ridgeway goes straight on (SU 213798), turn right to follow the permissive footpath signs to Liddington Castle.

As you go over the crest of the hill, the vast sprawling town of Swindon is laid out before you, as well as the nearby villages of Chiseldon, Liddington and Wanborough. Make your way to the viewing platform, where the old trig pillar has been supplemented by a viewpoint pillar, erected to mark the new Millennium. Although unexcavated, evidence shows that the ramparts of the hillfort were enlarged sometime during the Dark Ages, when foreign invaders were advancing across the country. Many regard this as the site of Mons Badonicus (or Mount Badon), a battle that allegedly took place around 495 AD between King Arthur and the Saxons. This was a lawless period in our history, with few recorded facts, so there has always been uncertainty about the location of many of the key events, or indeed precisely who was involved. Whatever the facts, the legend of King Arthur is a popular one, and it may well have started here, with a famous victory that brought a few years of peace to the region. Centuries later, peace can still be enjoyed on this isolated summit, and a young Richard Jefferies took advantage of it on many occasions.

Having inherited his father's love of literature and nature,

The ramparts on Liddington Hill

he wandered endlessly around the hills and fields, studying minute details of the countryside, and recording everything he saw. Here too he found inspiration for his writings, and on one of his regular pilgrimages to Liddington Hill he developed a sudden and uncontrollable urge to seek his destiny, his soul. To him it was like a vision of eternity, a burning desire to discover truth and understanding, a feeling he could not adequately describe in words:

> The inexpressible beauty of all filled me with a rapture, an ecstasy, he later wrote, 'I did not then define, or analyse, or understand this . . . I was utterly alone with the sun and the earth. Lying down on the grass, I spoke in my soul to the earth, the sun, the air, and the distant sea far beyond sight . . . the rich blue of the unattainable flower of the sky drew my soul towards it . . . I felt an emotion of soul beyond all definition.

Throughout *The Story of My Heart*, the long flowing passages blend seamlessly together as though written at the moment they actually occurred. Yet his words describe experiences from 17 years previously. When first published in 1883, this compelling book received hostile reviews, and was largely ignored by an unappreciative public, for it was far ahead of its time. Victorian society was not ready for this sort of material. Even now parts of it remain difficult to grasp, yet somehow the reader becomes engrossed in its powerful theme. Despite its controversial views on life, maybe even because of them, the book has been reprinted several times over the years.

Like so many of his contemporaries, Jefferies' talents and prophetic vision were not fully recognised until long after his untimely death in 1887, at the age of 38. Subsequently many have been inspired by him, and he was not the only writer to take Liddington Hill to heart. Alfred Williams and Charles Sorley were regular visitors, and both wrote poems about it, while H W Timperley was clearly attracted to more than the view:

> If any man's spirit found eternity on a hill-top, the spirit of Richard Jefferies found it here. For me there are two places where I feel the spiritual presence of men of genius who sought and discovered their greatest happiness in nature; one is Liddington Hill.

5 After visiting the castle, retrace your steps along the permissive path to the gate where you left the Ridgeway, and bear right to continue along it. Follow the obvious field edge path for 1500m to another gate, and go through it as indicated. After a further 300m a rutted track joins from the left, signed as Ridgeway route for vehicles (SU 215780). Turn here, almost 180 degrees, and follow this track all the way back to the B4192 near the layby.

Horses grazing above Shipley Bottom

Further reading:

Jefferies, Richard, various dates, *The Story of My Heart*
Thomas, Edward, 1978, *Richard Jefferies.* (Faber)
Looker, Samuel J & Porteous, Crichton, 1966, *Richard Jefferies, Man of the Fields.* (Country Book Club)
Massingham, H J, 1936, *English Downland.* (Batsford)

16 Names to Conjure with

Marlborough and Mildenhall

(6.25 miles/10 km) or **(4.5 miles/7.2 km)**

(OS Explorer 157)

Names and origins are an essential part of the history of many towns and villages, and none more so than the places that feature in this walk. Marlborough's coat of arms proudly displays the Latin motto 'Ubi nunc sapientis ossa Merlini', which translates as 'Where now are the bones of the wise Merlin?'. For according to legend it was Merlin, King Arthur's magician, who founded Marlborough and gave it the name 'Merlin's Borough'. However, not everyone agrees. Alternative theories exist, the most likely being that Marlborough means 'Maerla's Barrow' – the grave of

Marlborough High Street, flanked by the towers of its two churches, seen from Granham Hill

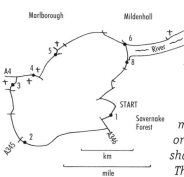

Maerla, who had some connection with a huge mound that rivalled Silbury Hill, and on which a castle was later built. Whatever the truth, at least the name Marlborough appears on the map – you will not find Werg or Minal, two other places we shall be visiting.

This walk passes many of the locations that have featured in Marlborough's well documented history. It combines quiet hill and riverside paths with the busy thoroughfares of the town centre, where there are ample opportunities to stop for refreshments. Look out too for the blue plaques that identify key events or places. A few short gradients have to be negotiated, with one fairly steep climb, and there are two main road crossings where you need to be careful of fast moving traffic.

1 Park at the picnic site just inside Savernake Forest on Postern Hill, accessed from the A346 (SU 198680). Walk back along the entrance drive to the main road, and turn left along the grass verge. For the best visibility, carry on to the end of the layby, then very carefully cross the road. Continue briefly along the opposite verge, then turn right into Brown's Farm. In the centre of the farmyard you will come to a gate beside a shed. Here a yellow arrow points straight on along a concrete road. Follow this road/track for almost a mile (1.6 km) until it drops downhill to an overgrown bridge under the tree-lined railway embankment (SU 182675).

This is the route of the former Marlborough branch line, built in 1864 to provide access to the west of England main line at Savernake Junction. It was Marlborough's only railway until 1881 when the rival M&SWJR line opened (see Chapter 4). The two routes operated side by side until 1933, when the branch line was abandoned. The M&SWJR line continued in use until 1964, and its tunnel, over which we have just walked, has since been converted into a bat sanctuary.

2 Go under the bridge to emerge on the A345 beside Granham Cottages. Carefully cross the road to the farm entrance opposite, where a footpath sign on the right-hand verge directs you to a stile and fence-lined path. Follow this path for 500m to another stile in trees on Granham Hill, overlooking Marlborough (SU 180680). Continue straight on to descend on a low bank beside a ditch. Go through a gap in the line of trees, and along the left-hand edge of the field. After the kissing gate, keep to the path beside the tennis courts, leading to the church car park. Follow the wall to enter the churchyard.

St George's church, Preshute

This is St George's church, Preshute, a particularly attractive building of chequered stonework. Inside is a large font made of black Tournai marble, one of only seven in the UK. Tradition claims that it was originally housed in the old castle chapel, where it was used to baptise King John's children. For Marlborough castle was once a royal residence, established by the Normans and occupied by successive monarchs for 400 years. In 1267 it was even the location for Henry III's parliament. The castle's popularity eventually waned, and by the 15th century it had become a ruin. Its final royal owner, Edward VI, bequeathed the property to his mother's family, and in its place a brick mansion was built in 1702. It remained the home of the Seymour family for the next 50 years.

3 Fork right through the churchyard to follow the tarmac path over the river and up to the Bath Road (A4). Turn right along the pavement, cross over, and continue along the opposite side towards the college arch.

In 1751 the Seymour house was converted into the Castle Inn, a quality establishment that soon gained a reputation as the finest coaching inn between London and Bath. At its peak in the early 19th century it serviced 40 coaches daily, but its prosperity quickly plummeted when the railways arrived. Almost overnight the coaching trade evaporated, and prospects for Marlborough looked bleak, especially as the railways had by-passed the town. But the end of one chapter in Marlborough's history heralded the start of another. With the Castle Inn no longer in business, the mansion was vacant. It was an ideal property for a public school, and in 1843 Marlborough College was born. Within five years it had become second only to Eton, and despite some early teething troubles, has since expanded significantly. As you pass the entrance gates, look across the open court to the prominent building on the far side. Now known as 'C House', this is the Seymour mansion/ Castle Inn. Nearby, the old mound, minus its castle, is enclosed by college buildings.

4 **Continue alongside the Bath Road, under the college arch, and around the corner to St Peter's church, redundant since 1974, and now a permanent craft centre and restaurant. Turn left to pass it on either side, and proceed along the left-hand side of the High Street.**

Always regarded as the widest in the country, Marlborough's High Street slopes gently, both from side to side, and from end to end. This prompts locals to refer to its 'top side, bottom side, top end and bottom end'. Hence our journey is along the 'top side' from 'bottom end' to 'top end'! The town is justifiably famous for its random mix of architectural styles, although much has changed over the centuries. In medieval times a row of timber houses and shops stood along the centre of the street, but all were destroyed when a disastrous fire swept through the town in 1653. Strong winds fanned the flames, and within three hours six people were dead, and 224 properties had been lost. Rebuilding began, but there were more fires over the next few years, leading eventually to a law forbidding the use of thatch.

5 **Continue to the top end of the High Street, and keep left of the town hall. Where the narrow road bends left, cross over into the alleyway beside the estate agents. Walk through to the churchyard and past St Mary's church, to emerge in The Green. On your left a blue plaque identifies the house where Nobel prize-winning author William Golding lived as a child. Follow the avenue of trees to the traffic lights, and cross the road (A346). Continue ahead**

into St Martins, signed as Ramsbury. Follow this road down Poulton Hill and out of town. Immediately after the river bridge, opposite the Rabley turning, cross the main road to the gateway where a sign points to Werg. Follow the grass path towards the distant mast, then climb the steps up to the old railway embankment (SU 201694).

6 To follow the 4.5 mile/7.2 km route, turn right along the railway embankment (cycle route 45) for about 400m, and rejoin the longer route at point 8. Otherwise, go over the embankment and down the other side. Keeping the various channels on your right, follow the riverside path to Mildenhall, with the church tower visible ahead. Go through the kissing gate and between the houses to emerge in front of the church, which has been praised by many for its rich interior furnishings. Walk up to the lychgate and through the churchyard, exiting by two kissing gates. Cross the field, parallel to the fence, aiming for another gate on the right of the sports pavilion. Carry straight on, to exit in the corner between hedge and fence. Turn right along the narrow lane to the river bridge (SU 215697).

This is Werg, a tiny hamlet with a name that seems to have no explanation. There were never more than nine houses here, although a mill existed until 1983 when it was destroyed by fire. Werg is really part of Minal, a name that developed as a local pronunciation of Mildenhall, although even this has been spelt dozens of different ways since it was first recorded in 803 AD as Mildenhald. Long before all of this it was *Cunetio*, an important Roman garrison at the junction of five main roads. Three separate settlements occupied the large field in front of you, as well as the hillside beyond, although no trace remains today, at least not above the surface. In the past many Roman relics have been unearthed, not least the discovery in 1978 of nearly 55,000 coins dating from the 3rd century – by far the largest hoard of its kind ever found in Britain.

7 Cross the river and follow the road around to pass a thatched cottage called The Bothy. As the road bends left, fork right alongside another thatched cottage, signed as footpath to Elcot. Keep to the riverside path until you reach a track junction beside a fenced-off river bridge. Fork right then immediately left between two posts where a yellow arrow points into a large field, facing the mast on the opposite hilltop. Follow the right-hand edge of the field

Marlborough seen from Granham Hill

all the way to the far end. When you reach the houses, go through a gap in the fir trees, to emerge on a concrete road beside the tile factory. Continue along the road to the railway bridge. In front of it, turn left along a rough tarmac road, as far as a gateway on your right, which allows access onto the railway cycle path (SU 202691). Re-join the short route here, and turn left.

Standing beside the cycle path is a green milepost, one of a thousand funded by the Royal Bank of Scotland to mark the creation of the National Cycle Network. Despite their name, they are not positioned at specific distances – the next one is just 500m further on!

8 The combined routes now follow the old railway path towards Marlborough as far as the next milepost, where the cycle route turns right to the town centre. Bear left here, signed as footpath to Savernake Forest, climbing steeply on a narrow chalk path. At the top is a T-junction with yellow arrows on a post. Turn right to follow the edge of the forest until you reach a wooden signpost (SU 196683). Turn sharp left around it, to enter the forest near a stile in a short section of fence. Finally, emerge from the trees into the open picnic site, directly opposite the parking area.

Further reading:

Chandler, Jess E., 2004, *A History of Marlborough*. (White Horse Bookshop)

Stedman, Alfred Redvers, 1960, *Marlborough and the Upper Kennet Country*. (Marlborough)

Besley, Edward, & Bland, Roger, 1983, *The Cunetio Treasure*. (British Museum)

Visit www.minal.org.uk for a more detailed history of Mildenhall

17 Dickens on the Downs
Martinsell, Oare, and Huish

(6 miles/9.6 km)

(OS Explorer 157)

Over the years Martinsell has received many accolades, all of which are fully justified. From the south its distinctive shape protrudes into the Vale of Pewsey, making it visible for many miles around. Approached from the north, however, it remains concealed until the very last moment, suddenly appearing through the trees as you arrive in the car park. For anyone who wants an easy stroll to a high vantage point with minimum effort, Martinsell is the ideal choice. Beyond the gate the view is magnetic, enticing you to climb to the top and stand on the summit of Wiltshire's third highest hill. This is just the start of the walk, which continues across the high ground, then descends steeply into Oare, and over fields to the tiny village of Huish. Along the way we shall pass two locations that feature in stories told by Charles Dickens, before tackling a steep climb back up to the hilltops for the return journey.
Choose springtime to see masses of bluebells and other wild flowers. Refreshments are available at the White Hart in Oare, and our walk ends with the opportunity to have a second look at everyone's favourite hill.

1 A small parking area is provided beside the minor road from Clench Common (SU 183645). Go through the gate and straight ahead alongside the wood. Where the wood ends, bear left up the grass path through trees, and follow it around as it climbs fairly steeply up to and along the contours of the old hillfort. Continue around the escarpment, past a gate and seat, then through trees where it may be muddy. Emerge into an open field (SU 176637) and proceed alongside the fence to a gate displaying a Mid-Wilts Way roundel.

Gateway to Martinsell Hill. The walk begins here.

The views across the Vale of Pewsey are extensive, and in common with other similar vantage points Martinsell was an ideal location for an Iron Age hillfort. Dating from around 1000 BC, and covering an area of 32 acres, its primary purpose was for enclosing cattle rather than defence, for the ramparts are fairly low. Over many centuries it was the site of various fetes and festivals, especially on Palm Sunday when many believed that mystical forces attracted them like an ancient magnet. It was probably just an excuse for a party, where men occupied themselves by fighting and drinking, while the children raced down the steep hillside using horses' skulls and jawbones as sledges.

2 Go through the gate to enter open access land, and walk along the top of the slope, keeping close to the fence on your right. Detour around a large group of gorse bushes, taking care not to descend more than is necessary. Return to the fence and stay beside it to the end, where a sunken track comes up steeply from the left as you approach a gate. As indicated by the Mid-Wilts Way arrow, go left of the gate to reach a signpost that points back to Martinsell (SU 171634).

The footpath heading off to the right passes close to the ruins of an old barn once used by a shepherd who lived here. His cottage, demolished in 1911, was certainly the highest inhabited building in Wiltshire, and is mentioned by Charles Dickens in *Household Words*, a periodical of miscellaneous literature he edited from 1850. According to a local informant, the shepherd's house was visible from the English Channel: '. . . they do say, them that's out at sea, mariners and such like, can see the very place we're standin' on; leastways the white house yon, top of Martin's Hill.'

On our left-hand side is an older and more obvious relic. Straddling the narrow ridge like a beached whale is a huge long barrow, where human remains have been unearthed. Although it shares its name with more than a dozen similar sites around the country, including one on the opposite side of the valley, few of them can compete with the outstanding location of this particular Giant's Grave. Surrounded on three sides by very steep slopes, it was an ideal spot for a Neolithic fortress, and nowadays it provides us with exceptional views on our walk, plus a challenge as we tackle the descent. On the left are overgrown strip lynchets similar to those encountered in Chapter 5.

3 From the Martinsell signpost, fork left to follow the fence along the ridge, directly towards the Giant's Grave. Cross the burial mound, and go past a trig pillar. Then descend very steeply, still beside the fence. At the bottom, look for a stile in the bushes. Fork left across the field and exit through a gate (SU 161628). Turn right along a wide track, signed as bridleway and Mid-Wilts Way. This becomes a tarmac lane and emerges on the A345 in Oare, a few steps from the White Hart Inn. Cross the road into Rudge Lane opposite. Shortly after going around a left-hand bend, look for a bridleway/footpath signpost on your right. Follow the bridleway past the house and stables, aiming for a gate and stile leading into an open field. Continue along the left-hand edge of the field, staying beside the fence to a gate in the far corner (SU 153631).

4 Exit the field at a junction near North Copse, where bluebells grow extensively in spring. Cross the stile in front of you, where a yellow arrow points into another field. Aim for the corner of the fence, then proceed alongside the wood. Go through a gate and over a stile, to continue along the edge of a second field. Ignore two gates in the corner, as you follow the field edge around until you reach a gate/

Steep descent from the Giant's Grave into Oare

stile near a house and stables (SU 147635). Drop down to the minor road and turn left along it. After passing a row of thatched cottages, turn right into the no through road. Just before the church is a pond on your right.

Another local story published by Dickens was borrowed from the *Piccadilly Annual* of 1848. Entitled 'The Ghost of Pit Pond', it recounts the tragic tale of Richard Reeves, a farmer who lived at Manor Farm, opposite Huish church. One summer evening in 1817 a runaway horse came galloping down the steep hill behind the farm. Its rider, a young lady called Miss Emily, was thrown from the saddle beside the village pond. Witnessing the incident, the farmer rushed to her aid, and immediately fell in love with her. She recovered, and they spent several days together before the farmer asked for her hand in marriage. But his proposal was rejected and Miss Emily vanished. Refusing to give up on her, the farmer embarked on a long search that finally ended months later in Belgium, where he discovered she had been badly treated and left to die in hospital. Distraught, he returned to Huish and took his own life in one of his barns. For some time afterwards terrified local residents saw his ghost wandering the lanes and fields, and eventually called on the parish priest to exorcise the spirit, appropriately laying it to rest in Pit Pond.

Nowadays this is a peaceful spot, and you will be tempted to linger, either to watch the ducks on the pond, or on the seat beside the church porch, where a past entry in the visitor's book reads quite simply: 'An oasis of peace and tranquillity'.

5 After visiting the church, return to the pond and go through the gate by the signpost to follow the gravel path around the perimeter of a private garden. Where the pond finishes, continue straight ahead along a narrow path between fence and hedgerow. At the end, emerge through a gap in the trees into a large open field. Turn left to pass an isolated building, and stay beside the fence as you head directly towards Huish Hill (SU 148641). At first the ascent is gradual, but the gradient increases significantly after you pass through the gate at the top of the field. The way ahead is straight up the ridged slope in front of you. This is open access land, so you are free to choose your own route to the top. Once there, take a breather, then fork right around the summit plateau to meet a fence, and follow it to a pair of gates in a corner, and another Mid-Wilts Way arrow (SU 151642).

At this point we are briefly reunited with the Mid-Wilts Way, and our route here also corresponds with two other named footpaths. The White Horse Trail is a 90-mile (145 km) circular trek that visits each of the county's white horses, while the Tan Hill Way is a 7-mile (11.2 km) linear route linking Wiltshire's three highest hills. The remainder of our journey follows the latter.

Huish church and Manor Farm

6 Turn right beside the wire fence, then cross the next field to another gate leading to a wide track through a young tree plantation. A sign here welcomes walkers. Exit the plantation onto a farm track at a bend near Huish Hill

House. Follow the track ahead around two more bends, then stay on it for the next 800m to reach the A345 (SU 164643).

7 Carefully cross the road onto the bridleway directly opposite, and follow this wide fence-lined track for 500m, until it ends at a gate (SU 169641). Fork left into the trees, and along a narrow ditch that is likely to be muddy, even in dry weather. This ancient earthwork runs along the southern edge of Withy Copse, a small wood that is full of bluebells and other wild flowers. At a crosstracks with 4-way signpost, continue ahead, signed as bridleway to Clench Common. Enter open access land at a gate (SU 177642), then fork left on a grass path that gradually descends around the rear of Martinsell Hill. Retrace your earlier steps back to the car park.

Charles Dickens enjoyed a good story, and often visited Wiltshire while researching his novels. Several locations around the county are featured in his books, although not all are obvious as some of the names have been changed. Subsequent writers tended to concentrate on the landscape itself, and although the downs offered ample choice, it was Martinsell that regularly appeared at the top of their list of favourites. In *The Vale of Pewsey*, H W Timperley helps us to understand why:

> Martinsell is a presence and a personality . . . it is one of those hills that take possession of the imagination from the start, one of the high places that all sorts of people like to visit and revisit or look for in the distance and recognise with pleasurable feelings that may not be easy to put into words for they spring, I think, from a deeper impulse than that which simply sends us to a hilltop to enjoy the exhilaration of height and a spacious view. We cannot forget the hill.

He was so impressed, he devoted an entire chapter to Martinsell, whereas H J Massingham was more succinct in his description: 'Martinsell spells Wiltshire', he wrote in *English Downland*. The final word, however, goes to Ken Watts, who in *The Marlborough Downs* simply calls it 'supreme'.

Further reading:

Alsop, James, 2007, *The Mid-Wilts Way*. (Ex Libris Press)
Massingham, H J, 1936, *English Downland*. (BT Batsford Ltd)
Timperley, H W, 1954, *The Vale of Pewsey*. (Robert Hale)

18 Along the Old Bath Road

Cherhill Down and Yatesbury

(7 miles/11.2 km) or (5 miles/8 km)

(OS Explorer 157)

Commanding extensive views from the top of Cherhill Down, the Lansdowne Monument is the most visible landmark in Wiltshire. Nearby, the same hilltop provides the most picturesque setting for one of the county's famous white horses. Less visible, but equally important in the county's history, is the route of the Old Bath Road, once used by royalty and celebrities of the day. Its successor, the A4, still carries travellers along the same journey, but as they speed past few will notice the old road higher up the hillside. Neither will they see the old airfield that once occupied the adjacent farmland. Our walk takes in all of these sights, and more. For the open terrain offers spectacular views that extend across many miles in all directions. Access is easy, thanks to the proximity of the A4, and although our route begins at a large parking area on Knoll Down, there are more laybys towards Cherhill that provide alternative starting points, if required. Most of the time we shall be following downland tracks and minor country lanes, although there are two short sections beside the A4, where vigilance is required crossing over. The climb up to Cherhill Down is fairly gentle, but a steep descent on the other side needs to be taken carefully. Chalk surfaces are especially slippery when wet, so I have deliberately avoided the path that descends further west, as it can be particularly treacherous. These gradients can be avoided by choosing the shorter route that bypasses the hill altogether.

1 Park in the large layby beside the A4, 1000m west of Beckhampton roundabout (SU 077692). This is a popular spot for dog walkers using the area around the adjacent gallops. At the top end of the layby is a bridleway sign pointing you towards a gate. Immediately bear right onto a grass path leading towards the clump of trees. There are several paths here, both through the wood and alongside it. The right of way then follows a rutted track between low banks, but another path runs parallel for some distance before they eventually merge into one. Keeping to the top of the ridge, walk in more or less a straight line, with the distinctive obelisk on Cherhill Down ahead of you, slightly to the left.

The Old Bath Road heading towards Cherhill Down

This is the course of the Old Bath Road, a highway that developed progressively over the centuries. When the Roman occupation ended in 410 AD, the hot springs at Bath fell into decline, as did much of the road network. More than a thousand years later Bath's popularity as a health resort began to re-emerge, encouraged by visits from Queen Anne and Elizabeth I. Yet by 1668, when Samuel Pepys made a well publicised trip, the condition of the roads had not improved. From London a new highway began to evolve by way of Reading and Newbury. From Hungerford different routes were tried, and at Beckhampton one headed towards Devizes before climbing over Beacon Hill, a notorious stretch where many coaches came to grief on the steep gradients. Because of this the route was later abandoned in favour of an alternative that followed the course of this walk over Cherhill Down. Until the turnpike system was developed there were few signs to show the way, and early maps offered only basic information. Consequently, many travellers hired local guides. At best, it was an uncomfortable 3-day coach journey from London to Bath; at worst,

The Lansdowne Monument

it was abandoned altogether or interrupted by highwaymen. Nevertheless, despite its hazards coach travel flourished. Seats were heavily over-subscribed, and by changing horses at regular intervals, a 2-day schedule was achieved in 1717. As the turnpike system progressed, the roads gradually improved, and in 1784 the first mail coach service ran from London to Bristol, offering security and punctuality. The idea rapidly caught on, and soon mail coaches became a familiar sight across the country. Although many of the old coaching roads have disappeared, a significant number of the milestones erected during the turnpike era still survive. The A4 between Newbury and Chippenham has an extensive collection. Many have been restored and repainted, including a fine example opposite the layby where this walk begins.

2 After 1.5 miles (2.4 km) we arrive at a T-junction with a wide chalk track (SU 055699). To follow the shorter route that bypasses the hill, turn right to the A4, and cross over near another layby. Walk to the junction and turn left towards Yatesbury. Follow the road as far as The Avenue, then turn right to rejoin the longer route at point 5. Otherwise, to continue with the longer route, turn left up the chalk track (Wessex Ridgeway). At the barn take the right-hand fork through the gate. Enter the National Trust land at the next gate, and continue on the sunken chalk track that climbs gradually up to Oldbury Castle hillfort. At the top, turn sharp right through a gap in the ramparts, aiming directly towards the Lansdowne Monument (SU 048693).

LANSDOWNE MONUMENT. This 38m high obelisk was built in 1845 by the Third Marquess of Lansdowne to commemorate his ancestor Sir William Petty (1623-87), a man of many talents who is chiefly remembered as a political economist. The monument was designed by Sir Charles Barry, who also worked on nearby Bowood House, the Lansdowne family home. After falling into disrepair, it was renovated by the National Trust in 1991, and its tiered base is a popular spot for walkers to rest and admire the very extensive views.

3 Arriving at the monument, turn sharp right in front of it, to follow the grass path along the top of the steep escarpment, as it curves around and goes over the top of the white horse. The hillside then descends steeply, and may be slippery when wet. At the bottom, exit the National Trust land at a gate and cattle grid, and follow the track through the trees to the A4 (SU 046702).

CHERHILL WHITE HORSE. Occupying the most picturesque setting of any Wiltshire hill carving, the Cherhill white horse was cut in 1780 by Dr Christopher Allsop, a resident of Calne who was nicknamed 'the mad doctor'. The design of the county's first white horse at Westbury had not been without its critics, so Dr Allsop may well have been inspired to create something more graceful for his neighbours to admire. Using a megaphone from a vantage point some distance away, he shouted instructions to his workmen as they marked out the shape on the hillside. The turf was then cut away and replaced by chalk from a quarry on the hilltop. In common with other hill figures, the horse needs regular maintenance. In his 1857 book *The Scouring of the White Horse*, Thomas Hughes explained how the white horse at Uffington was traditionally restored every 7 years, usually accompanied by local festivities. With musicians and acrobats in attendance, plus plenty of free-flowing ale, it's hardly surprising that such events were well patronised. In 1780 one newspaper even claimed an attendance of 30,000! At Cherhill fresh chalk was added every few years from the hilltop quarry, by lowering it in trucks down the steep slope. In 1876 one of the trucks broke free and hurtled down the hillside, narrowly missing one of the workmen. The wheel tracks made by the heavily laden trucks remained visible for some while afterwards, often filling up with chalk after heavy rain. At times, therefore, the horse appeared to be mounted on stilts! Nowadays fresh chalk is flown in by helicopter.

4 Carefully cross over the A4 and turn left along the pavement. In front of the speed limit signs is a signpost pointing towards Jugglers Lane. Just beyond is a layby that may provide an alternative starting point for this walk. Turn here, towards Jugglers Lane. Passing farm buildings, go through the gate ahead of you, then ignore the first track on the right. A few steps further on is a T-junction beside a byway signpost that also mentions National Cycle Route No 4. Turn right along the rough gravel track, and follow it all the way to Yatesbury.

This section takes us along the perimeter of the former airfield, whose military history dates back to 1916. Since then thousands of RAF personnel were trained here, including Wing Commander Guy Gibson, VC, leader of the famous Dambusters Squadron. He was one of the first recruits to attend a new flying school that opened in 1936 amid claims that it was the best in the country. When war broke out three years later, the base expanded, and Tiger Moths became a familiar sight in the skies as novice pilots hastily notched up their flying hours ready for battle. To protect the base, air-raid shelters were dug, anti-aircraft guns installed, and pillboxes constructed around the airfield. Three of them still stand beside the track, plus another in the adjacent field, its roof covered with a thick layer of turf to conceal it from the air. Since closure in 1969, much of the airfield has been returned to farmland, although some of the old buildings remain and are now being redeveloped.

5 Emerge onto Norlands Road opposite the Old Rectory, and turn right to the junction, where we meet the shorter route head on. Turn left into The Avenue, still signed as National Cycle Route No 4. Go past the church and Back Lane, then before the junction with The Street,

look for a byway sign on the verge beside a telegraph pole
(SU 066715). Turn right onto a wide rutted track and follow
it for precisely one mile (1.6 km) to a byway crossroads
beneath a small group of trees (SU 077703).

Over to the left is Windmill Hill, the earliest part of the
Avebury complex. Although now just a low grass-covered hill,
it was built as a causewayed camp by the Neolithic people who
lived here around 3,700 BC. Apart from the burial mounds little
evidence is now visible.

6 To visit Windmill Hill, turn left at the byway crossroads.
Otherwise, turn right to Cooks Plantation on the A4, then
left along the narrow pavement to return to the layby.
Carefully cross the road on reaching the milestone.

The Lansdowne Monument and Cherhill White Horse

Further reading:

Marples, Morris, 1991, *White Horses and other hill figures.* (Alan
    Sutton)
Berryman, David, 2002, *Wiltshire Airfields in the Second World
    War.* (Countryside Books)
Phillips, Daphne, 1983, *The Great Road to Bath.* (Countryside
    Books)
Roberts, Cecil, 1940, *And So To Bath.* (Hodder & Stoughton)

19 In the Footsteps of our Ancestors
Avebury and Silbury Hill

(5.5 miles/8.8 km)

(OS Explorer 157)

Avebury needs no introduction. Its stone circle attracts thousands of visitors each year, and many prefer it to Stonehenge. Unlike its famous neighbour further south, there are no restrictions on walking among the many stones, no queuing at peak times, and no admission charges. But Avebury is much more than just the largest stone circle in Europe. It represents a World Heritage Site that also includes Silbury Hill, the Sanctuary, and West Kennett Long Barrow. This walk visits each of these prehistoric monuments, allowing time to inspect them in detail, and thus provides us with tantalising reminders of our Neolithic ancestry.

1 Start at the main pay and display car park on the A4361 Beckhampton Road in Avebury (SU 100696). Normally there is ample space here, but peak times can be busy, and it should be avoided in mid-June, when thousands descend on Avebury to celebrate the summer solstice. At such times, consider joining the walk on Overton Hill – see later. A path leads to the stone circle and village street.

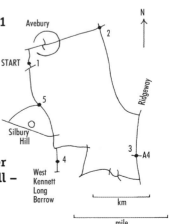

Turn right to the main road where it forms a double bend, overlooked by the Red Lion pub. On the opposite side is Green Street, the Old London Way coach road we encountered in Chapter 2. For vehicles this is a no through road. Follow it out of the village, and through the outer bank of the great circle. The tarmac ends at Manor Farm (SU 111703).

2 Just after the farm is a byway crossing. Turn right, signed to Overton Hill. This is a wide rutted track that may well be muddy, especially at the outset. As you progress, look down to the right to see the line of standing stones that leads out of Avebury along Stone Avenue. The track now climbs gradually up to a beech clump, then meets the Ridgeway at a T-junction (SU 119688). Turn right to descend to the A4, where there is a small parking area.

This is Overton Hill, otherwise known as Seven Barrows Hill, for obvious reasons. Approaching from the north, the horizon is dominated by the smooth undulating outline of Wiltshire's highest summits. In the foreground, the layout of the barrows seems to mimic the distant hills, their flowing shapes merging seamlessly into each other. Maybe our ancestors intended to create a mirror image.

Arriving at the A4, we have also reached the southern end of the Ridgeway national trail that began 87 miles (139 km) away on Ivinghoe Beacon in Buckinghamshire. From this point the Ancient Ridgeway continued south across the Vale of Pewsey and onto Salisbury Plain. Its modern footpath equivalent – the Wessex Ridgeway – takes a different route. Beginning in Marlborough, this 137-mile (219 km) long distance footpath follows the Old London Way into Avebury, then aims for Devizes and Westbury, before continuing all the way to the Dorset coast at Lyme Regis, where the Ancient Ridgeway may also have ended.

> THE SANCTUARY. On the opposite side of the A4 is an enclosed area of grass, with assorted concrete blocks apparently scattered all around. This was a religious or ceremonial site that may well be older than Avebury's stone circle. One theory suggests that it was an interim resting place for the dead, prior to final interment in one of the nearby long barrows. Originally it consisted of six concentric circles of wooden posts, probably supporting a roof. Several centuries later the posts were replaced by a double stone circle, linked to Avebury by an avenue of

stones that represented a processional highway. This arrangement survived until the early 18th century when it was visited by William Stukeley, an antiquarian who has since been described as 'Britain's most observant field archaeologist'. It seems he arrived just in time to record the scene for posterity, for in 1724 the hillside was unceremoniously ploughed up by the local farmer, probably urged on by the church, who regarded such places as pagan. As a result the Sanctuary disappeared until 1930 when it was re-discovered and excavated by Maud Cunnington, using Stukeley's sketches.

3 Very carefully cross the A4. Visibility is not good here, and fast traffic can appear suddenly. After visiting the Sanctuary, follow the adjacent byway downhill past another barrow. At the bottom, where the track bends left to cross the river, turn right through a gateway indicated by a blue arrow on the post. Follow the field edge, which may be waterlogged when the river is high. Exiting onto a minor road, turn left over the bridge, then immediately go right on a byway between two paddocks. This too may be muddy or waterlogged at times. Continue ahead as far as two large barns (SU 110677), and turn right along the narrow road. Just before the river bridge, turn left onto a signed footpath, over a stile, and straight on beside the fence. On reaching a solitary oak tree where you meet the end of a gravel path, turn left uphill on a wide grass strip between open fields to visit West Kennett Long Barrow (SU 105678).

West Kennett Long Barrow

WEST KENNETT LONG BARROW. This was a burial place for more than a thousand years, before it was finally sealed by the massive sarsen slabs that still stand here as a tribute to the skills of those who somehow managed to drag them into position using little more than their bare hands. When excavated in 1955 the remains of 46 bodies were discovered, plus various artefacts. Take a torch if you wish to inspect the interior. This is a lonely windswept place, and knowing its ancient purpose, you would be forgiven for feeling uneasy about being here alone. Nevertheless, you may wish to pause for a few moments to soak up the atmosphere, and to speculate how many of our ancestors stood on this very spot, gazing out across the same landscape, albeit with quite a few more trees in the scene than there are today.

4 Retrace your steps to the oak tree, and turn left along the path to re-cross both the river and the A4. For a closer look at Silbury Hill, follow the pavement and continue to the car park beyond the hill. At the back of the car park look for a bridleway arrow pointing along a fence-lined grass path. This rejoins the main route at a river bridge (SU 101689). This diversion will add 800m to your journey.

SILBURY HILL. Of all the units that make up the Avebury complex, Silbury Hill is the most visible, and the most mysterious. Why it was built, and how it fits into the overall picture, remain a mystery. Constructed in stages between 2,300 and 2,000 BC, its timing seems to coincide with the sealing of West Kennett Long Barrow. But are the two events connected? Early

Silbury Hill and the infant River Kennet

theories explained it as a gigantic tomb, where a certain King Sil was buried. Such suggestions were supported by sightings of his ghost riding his horse around it! Now-adays we may think otherwise, although we are still no closer to a definitive explanation. Since 1776 several investigations have probed the hill's secrets. All failed, but one thing is certain. Regular tunnelling into the depths of Europe's largest prehistoric mound substantially weakened the structure. Inadequate backfilling of the various shafts created a number of internal voids that periodically collapsed. In May 2000 the central shaft opened up, leaving a crater on the summit. Further collapses followed, and before any remedial work could begin a detailed geophysical survey had to be under-taken to identify the cavities. With this information, extensive repair work was carried out in 2007-8 to ensure that this unique structure remains safe for future generations to ponder over.

5 **To bypass Silbury Hill, go through the gate signed Avebury Avenue, and follow the river directly ahead. Meet up with the diverted route at the river bridge (SU 101689), then continue straight on to exit onto the A4361 opposite the car park entrance.**

THE SCOTTISH CONNECTION. When the electronics company Marconi announced its intention to erect a radio mast on Windmill Hill in 1923, conservationists and the local community were outraged. For this sacred site is where the Avebury legend was born. Campaigners enlisted the support of Alexander Keiller, heir to the Dundee marmalade fortune. Marconi's plans were subsequently rejected, but Keiller purchased the land for excavation, and by 1929 had unearthed the largest Neolithic settlement in Europe. He went on to purchase Avebury itself, with the intention of re-creating the stone circle, using the sketches made by William Stukeley in the early 18th century. During the Middle Ages many of the huge sarsens had been toppled over or buried in deep pits, largely on the instructions of the church. Others had been cut up for building. Few remained intact, although one defied all attempts to remove it. Weighing 60 tons, the Swindon Diamond Stone still stands in its original position, and can be seen right beside the main road. Until war brought Keiller's work to a premature end in 1939, he succeeded in lifting many of the buried stones and resetting them in concrete. Missing stones were marked by small pillars. Much more recently, geophysical surveys have identified the locations of several more stones still lying buried beneath the surface. Perhaps that continuing air of mystery has helped to make Avebury the place it is today. As Sir John Betjeman once described it, - 'a haunting place to see at all times and in all weathers.'

Further reading:

Meaden, Terence, 1999, *The Secrets of the Avebury Stones.* (Souvenir Press)
Burl, Aubrey, 2002, *Prehistoric Avebury.* (Yale University Press)
Ucko, P J & others, 1991, *Avebury reconsidered.* (Unwin Hyman)

The Swindon Diamond Stone at Avebury

20 Top of Wiltshire

The Wansdyke from Tan Hill to Milk Hill

(6.25 miles/10 km)

(OS Explorer 157)

No book about walking in this part of Wiltshire would be complete without a visit to one of the very best walking locations in southern England. Add to that centuries of ancient history, and you have a day out to remember. For years the Wansdyke has been a constant topic for discussion and debate, yet its true origins still remain uncertain. Who built it? Why, and when? We think we know some of the answers, but we can never be quite sure about the precise facts. One thing is certain, however. This whole area is spectacular scenery, and for our final walk we shall be taking a more intimate look at this enigmatic earthwork, before ending on a real high. The landscape here is remote and exposed to the elements. The ground is uneven in places, and some of the gradients are fairly steep. Nearest refreshments are the Barge Inn at Honeystreet, or the Kings Arms in All Cannings.

1 Start at the Knap Hill car park, beside the Alton Barnes – Lockeridge road (SU 116638). On the opposite side of the road is a gate and stile. Enter the field and, keeping the fence on your left, proceed straight ahead, level at first, then after an intermediate gate, climbing steadily up to the ridge.

Reminders of the Saxon period are all around us. Our path is the Workway Drove, more recently used for moving cattle, but originally a Saxon *weorc-weg* or 'way by the stronghold'. This refers to Knap Hill, the distinctive mound that supports a Neolithic causewayed camp dating from around 3,500 BC. Although built primarily for ceremonial purposes, its elevated position made it ideal as a defended settlement.

Then just before reaching a third gate, our route takes us past a settlement known to the Saxons as *Eald Burh* or 'Old Town'. A short distance away on our left-hand side, and passed later in our walk, is Oxenmere, a dewpond referred to in the Anglo Saxon Charter of 825 AD as *Oxnamere*. More Saxon evidence awaits as we progress, primarily, of course, the Wansdyke itself, which is now clearly visible in front of us.

2 Go through the third gate, and proceed to the gap in the Wansdyke bank (SU 107646). Turn left through another gate displaying a yellow arrow, and follow the track parallel to the bank. The two come together within 400m at the start of a rough tarmac track, alongside a Pewsey Downs National Nature Reserve notice. Remember this location for later (SU 102647).

3 Continue along the rough tarmac for a short distance to the next junction, where another track comes in from the right. Climb up to the stile in front of you, to gain access to the bank, waymarked as Mid-Wilts Way.

Ahead of you, the huge undulating bank of the Wansdyke stretches away into the distance, all the time clinging to the

Looking towards Tan Hill from Milk Hill

contours of Tan Hill, before finally turning and disappearing over the top. This location is as dramatic as any you will find in southern England. Remote from roads and modern life, it can be silent and peaceful in calm conditions, but totally wild and inhospitable when lashed by wind and rain. Many believe that to fully appreciate its role in British history, you should experience it in all its moods, and in all weathers. After all, our ancestors had no choice. But who were they, and why did they spend so much time digging a massive earthwork in this hostile terrain. Over the years many theories have been put forward, and to assess their credibility we have to recall the history of the period.

Following the departure of the Romans, Britain was left without any form of central government, and therefore an easy target for a takeover bid. Soon prospective Saxon invaders were crossing the channel, and met little resistance as they infiltrated the east of the country. So it is reasonable to conclude that the Wansdyke was created at about this time by the Britons living in the south. This would date it to the late 5th century. However, in 495 AD a rival Saxon army landed on the south coast, and began advancing north. So were they responsible for building the Wansdyke to guard their newly acquired territory against their fellow countrymen? After all, the name Wansdyke is clearly of Saxon origin – from *Wodnesdic*, the ditch of Woden, the Saxon god of war. With no detailed records to guide us, we cannot be sure, although the layout of the bank and ditch proves that it was built to defend against an attack from the north. Many believe that it once extended all the way from the Severn Estuary to Savernake Forest, which at the time would have been impenetrable. In the west, much of the evidence to support this idea has been lost, but the surviving 10-mile section from Morgan's Hill to West Woods is indisputable, as it carves out a gigantic furrow across the downland slopes and ridges.

Writing in 1953, archaeologist O G S Crawford declared that there was '. . . no finer downland in the whole of England.' L V Grinsell agreed, nominating the Wansdyke as '. . . one of the most spectacular experiences in British field archaeology.' As you continue with this walk, you will find it hard to disagree.

4 Follow the Wansdyke bank for 1900m, taking care to avoid the many rabbit holes in the surface, and exposed patches of chalk, some of which are unstable. The parallel track on the left of the bank may be more convenient, and will help to reduce further erosion. The highest point is

Walking the Wansdyke towards Tan Hill

reached at another gap in the bank, where a small cluster of trees surrounds a gate and stile. Numerous waymarkers point in all directions (SU 083651). Without going through the gate, turn sharp left to follow the fence, now climbing to the summit of Tan Hill, which is marked by a trig pillar in the field on your right.

To the north, the views range from Morgan's Hill, with its twin masts, across Cherhill Down and the Lansdowne Monument, past Silbury Hill, Hackpen and the Ridgeway, and eastwards to Savernake Forest. On the other side, the Vale of Pewsey is laid out before us, ending abruptly at the northern escarpment of Salisbury Plain. Some days you will be totally alone in this wild and dramatic landscape, interrupted only by the happy song of a skylark, hovering in the still air, or the mewing call of a buzzard, drifting in the thermals high above. When the wind blows, when mist covers the valley, or when a black sky threatens to drench everything in sight, you begin to appreciate the untamed environment that our ancestors faced on a daily basis, as they strove to defend their territory against hostile invaders.

TAN HILL. Despite the uncertainties of the weather in this bleak spot, it was a popular attraction for many on one day each year. Hilltop fairs were common in past centuries, and Tan Hill was no exception. Originally called St Anne's Hill, for more than 500 years it was the venue for a fair on 6th August – St Anne's Day. As well as a stock fair that attracted farmers from far and wide, it was also a social occasion, and something of a public holiday. After the farming business had been concluded, the ale flowed freely, and the celebrations lingered well into the night. Some of those attending may well have been responsible for developing a local tale about a donkey that was supposedly carved into the lower slopes of the hill. Maybe it was intended as a rival to the white horse across the valley, although from the little we know of its existence, it seems to have been a totally different sort of creature. Legend claims that when the church bell in All Cannings struck midnight, the donkey came down to drink from the pond at Cannings Cross! At least that part of the story was probably concocted by late night revellers. Despite a plausible sighting reported by author Kathleen Wiltshire in her 1975 book *Wiltshire Folklore*, the donkey itself has since disappeared without trace, and even its precise location remains uncertain.

5 Shortly after passing the summit pillar we reach a gate, where a notice explains about the open access land beyond, approved under the Defra farm conservation schemes. (See Chapter 5 for more details of Conservation Walks). Access here is currently valid until September 2013. Go through the gate and bear slightly left onto a downhill grass path, with the earthworks around Rybury Camp directly in front of you. At the bottom, go through the gate (SU 083641), turn left beside the fence, then follow the contours of the hillside around to cut off the corner. On the other side, bear right alongside the fence, to drop down into a hollow at the base of Clifford's Hill, which now towers above. Turn left with the fence, and after 400m exit by a gate onto a wide farm road, where there are notices about hang-gliding (SU 090639).

6 Turn left along the farm road, which is clearly visible ahead climbing steeply up the hillside, to the rear of the Milk Hill escarpment. At the top we rejoin the Wansdyke and retrace our earlier footsteps along the rough tarmac track to the nature reserve notice (SU 102647). Beside the notice is a small gate, with Mid-Wilts Way and White Horse Trail roundels. Do not go through the gate. Instead, look to the left of it, where the tarmac ends, to locate a gap in the low bank beside a Conservation Walks notice. Follow the permissive path along the edge of the field, keeping the fence on your right, and past a horse jump. Continue past a second horse jump, where the fence curves right, then a few steps later (SU 103644), turn left on a wide grass strip between fields. There are no signs here – if you reach the third horse jump you have gone too far.

> MILK HILL. There are no signs to tell you that this is the highest point in Wiltshire. As you cross the bare hilltop plateau, the summit is reached when you draw level with the reservoir tank. Pause here to savour the moment, and enjoy more far-reaching views. Until a few years ago, Milk Hill and Tan Hill were awarded equal status, each topping 294m above sea level. Recent re-measuring, however, has shown Milk Hill to be taller by just a few inches, rounded up to 295m.

7 Continue across the hilltop and downhill to the field boundary on the other side. Turn right along the field edge, and go past Oxenmere dewpond in the trees (SU 106641). At the bottom follow the field edge around to a small gate and stile beside another Countryside Walks notice. Fork left, descending to another gate, halfway along a fence. Continue along the contours, and over the top of the fence that surrounds the Alton Barnes white horse.

Walking the Wansdyke towards Milk Hill, the highest point in Wiltshire

8 Follow the narrow path around the hillside and through some gorse bushes. Where the track forks, go right to climb up to Adam's Grave, or left to bypass it. Look for a stile in the fence, then aiming for the car park, cross two more fields to emerge on the road.

ADAM'S GRAVE. This is Walker's Hill, named not with pedestrians in mind but after Clement Walker, a former landowner. Its prominent position overlooking much of the Vale of Pewsey is further enhanced by the large Stone Age burial chamber on its summit. Locals still refer to it as 'Old Adam', but the Saxons called it *Wodnesbeorg*, or Woden's Barrow. Because of the strategic importance of this location two major battles were fought in the vicinity in 592 and 715 AD, both involving Saxon armies. Our walk ends with an optional climb to the top, although really the opportunity should not be missed, for it offers a splendid vantage point, and perhaps somewhere to sit and ponder as our journey draws to a close.

Further reading:

Grinsell, Leslie V, 1958, *The Archaeology of Wessex*. (Methuen)
Crawford, O G S, 1960, *Archaeology in the Field*. (London)
Timperley, H W, 1954, *The Vale of Pewsey*. (Robert Hale)
Chandler, John, 2000, *The Vale of Pewsey*. (Ex Libris Press)

Hobnob Press publishes or distributes a range of books for walkers and visitors to the region, which are available from booksellers or directly from the publisher. Uniform with this volume is:

Footsteps: the Cream of South Wiltshire Walks, edited by John Chandler (2002, £6.95, paperback, ISBN 0946418306). *Seventeen walks across South Wiltshire chosen by country writers and experts on various aspects of the Wiltshire countryside, including Chris Cole.*

For further information visit our website:
www.hobnobpress.co.uk
or write for a catalogue to:
Hobnob Press, PO Box 1838, East Knoyle, Salisbury SP3 6FA